COMICS
THE BEGINNING COLLECTOR

COMICS
THE BEGINNING COLLECTOR

VINCENT CECOLINI
AND
JOHN NUBBIN

MALLARD
PRESS

An imprint of
BDD Promotional Book Company, Inc.
666 Fifth Avenue
New York, New York 10103

A FRIEDMAN GROUP BOOK

Published by MALLARD PRESS
An imprint of BDD Promotional Book Company, Inc.
666 Fifth Avenue
New York, New York 10103

Mallard Press and its accompanying design and logo are trademarks of
BDD Promotional Book Company, Inc.

ISBN 0-792-45476-6

THE BEGINNING COLLECTOR: COMICS
was prepared and produced by
Michael Friedman Publishing Group, Inc.
15 West 26th Street
New York, NY 10010

Designer: Judy Morgan
Photography Editor: Ede Rothaus

Vintage comic books from the Robert Pistella collection.
All other comics are from the collections of Vincent Cecolini and C. J. Henderson.

Photography by John Gruen

Silhouettes: pp. 6–7; Batman, D.C. Comics; p.11: Captain America, Marvel Comics; p.23: Hawkworld,
D.C. Comics; p.37: Sam & Max, Comico, p.45: Superman, D.C. Comics; p.51: Walt Disney's Comics,
Dell Comics; p.65: Batman, D.C. Comics; p.71: The New Mutants, Marvel Comics; p.81: Flash Comics,
D.C. Comics; p.89: Weird Fantasy, Entertaining Comics; p.97: Spiderman: Marvel Comics; p.101:
Teenage Romances; p.109: Entertaining Comics

Typeset by: Classic Type, Inc.
Color separations by: Excel Graphic Arts Company
Printed and bound in Hong Kong by: Leefung-Asco Printers Ltd.

Acknowledgements

The authors would like to thank the following people for their help in completing this book: John Hunter, Gary Esposito, Tony Kibort, Jeff Rosoff (Manhattan Comics and Cards), and C. J. Henderson.

Dedication

This book is dedicated to Stan, Jack, Alan, Frank, Bill, and the many others who have made reading and collecting comic books worthwhile.

CONTENTS

Introduction

You've been reading comic books for quite awhile, enjoying the adventures and tribulations of characters like Superman and Batman, Spider-Man, and Wolverine. You've begun to appreciate the work of artists like Bill Sienkiewicz and Jack Kirby and writers like Alan Moore and Neil Gaiman. Your interest has developed to the point where the selection at your neighborhood newsstand no longer satisfies your needs.

You've even sought out your local comic book specialty shop. Once inside, you were amazed at the variety of titles, formats, and genres available. Some of the customers and shop dealers are on a first name basis with each other. The lingo spoken between them is foreign to you. The atmosphere makes you feel as if you've stepped into another world, and you have—the rarefied world of the comic book collector.

All around you people are buying—sometimes for substantial amounts—back issues of comics you've purchased at your local newsstands for pocket change. Your interest has been piqued. Now you want to learn how you can go about earning easy cash for your comic books; you too, want to collect comic books for profit. Trading, selling, and becoming rich—what could be easier? Right?

Wrong. It's an old saying, but a true one—if it were easy, everyone would be doing it. You'll be entering one of the most volatile hobbies around. Books, highly prized one day, can become worthless overnight. No one can guarantee you success as a comic collector, but you can believe that anyone who puts his or her heart and soul into the business of collecting, anyone who really works at it, will continually be fulfilled, never bored, and most important, will have fun.

In this book you'll discover just what comic books are:

their physical makeup, various formats, and genres. A grading system will be discussed to enable you to determine the condition and price of your books and what is actually worth paying for a book you might wish to add to your collection. You will be able to plot your own strategies about buying costly back issues. This book covers proper care of your comics, where and how you should buy and sell, as well as a host of other topics.

But first, realize that you have made the initial step toward entering one of the best hobbies around. Unlike baseball cards or stamps, both of which can only be glanced at from time to time, comic books are not merely trophies to be tracked down and tucked away. They can be read over and over.

Comics can be entertaining and enlightening. Some are funny, some are exciting, some are even intellectually challenging. Whatever the case, though, the bottom line is to have fun first and worry about profit second. After all, a collection should never be judged by its size, but rather by how much enjoyment the owner got out of collecting it in the first place.

Note: The prices listed throughout this book are not exact or current market prices and should not be used as guides for the purchase or sale of any comics. Although the prices were correct at the time this book was composed, the prices listed here should be used only as examples and guides to learning the comic book market. In order to get current prices to update the value of a collection, haggle for a sales price, or price an item for resale, collectors should consult the latest issues of the various price guides as well as the specialty shops they frequent.

No. 25

Action Comics

JUNE

10¢

Action Comics No. 1 *introduced the world to Superman, the first costumed super-hero. Created by teenagers Jerry Siegel and Joe Shuster, the character revolutionized the comics industry, making way for a multitude of super-heroes.*

O ver the years, for many, comic books have become the ultimate form of escape. In a time when we lack legends, myths, or even a standard grouping of tall tales, they, more than even television or movies, have become our system of the fantastic—our way of leaving all cares behind. For decades now, the big and small screen have concentrated on becoming the world's new "literature," addressing the world's shared problems. Whenever films like *Rambo* or television series such as *Miami Vice* come along, stressing individuality or moral responsibility, they are called candy for the mind, or visual comic books, as though that is a negative label. But comics are practically the only places left where moral les-

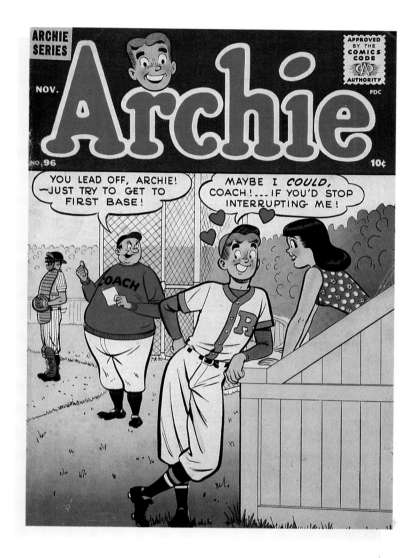

Archie, *and the numerous Archie off-shoot titles have continued to offer light-hearted humor with a social message since the early 1940s. The Archie Series is one of the few lines of comic books to appeal to a female, as well as a male, audience.*

sons are available to us and our children. Whether Superman is duking it out with Alien Invaders from outer space, or Pop Tate is explaining life to Archie and Jughead down at the malt shoppe, comics are still pretty much involved with the "big lesson"—it's better to be good than bad, bullies must be stopped (understand them if it helps, but stop them first before they go too far), one has to take responsibilities for one's actions, and so forth.

Blue noses and cranks, however, constantly on the lookout for ways to tell people what to do and how to avoid responsibility for their actions, have attacked comics viciously for the past fifty years, accusing them of fostering every kind of crime and delinquency under the sun.

1897
Richard Outcault's *Yellow Kid*, which appeared in the *New York American News*, is the first strip to be released in a reprinted collection, creating, in essence, the first comic book.

A DAY LIKE ANY OTHER.

5.

The consistently funny Reid Fleming: World's Toughest Milkman, written and drawn by David Boswell, is one of the few surviving black and white comics (a curious, colorless medium which relies on just pencils and inks).

1933
Harry Wildenberg and Max C. Gaines begin printing "tabloid-size" reprint books of Sunday newspaper strips for Proctor and Gamble to be given away as premiums. With the success of these books, Eastern Color Printing begins publishing similar books for other companies to use as giveaways.

The attacks have come and gone, and will come and go again. It makes no difference; comics are here to stay, because like television and unlike cigarettes, they ultimately can have good effects. Indeed, so many generations have learned their moral ABCs from the comics that they have become a part of our everyday vocabulary.

What makes a comic book a comic book? Today, comic books have progressed into so many different shapes, sizes, styles, genres, and formats that it is impossible to just call them comic books. As industry pioneer Will Eisner has said, "How can you call it a comic book? Comic means humorous and most are not funny."

But no matter the story line, standard-size, mainstream

Badger, *written by Mike Barron, is noted for its off-beat super-hero action. Like most adventure-oriented comics, each page is broken down into panels whose size varies for specific effects: smaller panels used for tight close-ups, larger panels used for wider shots, etc.*

comic books are all composed of shiny paper front and back covers, with various degrees of white paper in between; the pages contain any number of panels depending on what the artist and writer call for. Sometimes there can be a splash (one large panel filling an entire page) or a double splash (one panel spread across two pages).

The panels are comprised of a writer's plot or script broken down by the artist. Once the story and art are finalized by the editor, the artist's panels will be lettered, then inked.

The letterer places the necessary words, balloons, and boxes first to save the inker time, because any space com-

> **1934**
> Eastern Color Printing issues *Famous Funnies, Series No. 1* for Dell Publishing Company. It sells out immediately after hitting the newsstands in May, 1934. First issue price: ten cents.

The Sandman, DC's innovative horror title uses color to build not only traditional atmosphere and emotion, but a sense of fear and pain as well. This is a good series for adult collectors, because it has intelligent themes and sophisticated story lines.

1935

The first comic from National Periodical Publications (later to be known as DC Comics), *New Fun Comics*, is released.

1936

National Periodical Publications, deciding to switch the direction of *New Fun Comics* from humor, adventure, and detective stories to adventure, changes the book's name to *More Fun.*

manded by a word balloon or box does not have to be inked. Art that, for whatever reason, must be inked before it is lettered causes special problems. All the lettering must be cut out and pasted onto the art, and this is a long, involved process that does not guarantee that some of the lettering might not fall off before it reaches the printer. Inkers embellish the penciled artwork with black ink to detail each panel to reflect textures and lighting, as well as for printing purposes.

Then, finally, it is the colorist's turn. Four different colors of ink are used to print comics: black, red, blue, and yellow. Used on white paper in varying degrees, combinations and gradations, they are the only colors needed to

Batman: Legends of the Dark Knight, *the first new Batman title in over forty years, is an example of a series within a series. The storyline is treated like a miniseries, with the complete story unfolding over five or six issues that are each written and drawn by a different creative team. (Series-within-a-series titles are usually collected and published in graphic album form later on.)*

create all the colors in every comic you see (though this process is changing as computers become the main tool of the colorist).

COMIC FORMATS

All comic books currently on the market, no matter what the format, are produced as stated above or with some minor variations. These are not important for our purposes, however. What we need to do is look at the different formats available today.

LIMITED SERIES
A title that will only be run for a specific, predetermined number of issues. These

1936
With the success of *Famous Funnies*, other publishers, in conjunction with major newspaper syndicates, begin flooding the market with reprint books. Among these new books is *Wow Comics*, featuring early art from Will Eisner and Bob Kane, soon to become the creators of the Spirit (Eisner) and Batman (Kane).

Spider-Man, *Marvel Comics'* trademark character, has recently enjoyed a revival of popularity. Part of that revival can be credited to the return of many classic foes he faced off against early in his career. Note the similarity in style and color used in the first appearance of the Molten Man in an early issue of the Amazing Spider-Man *and then in his return in a recent issue of* Web of Spider-Man.

range from the one-shot, to the miniseries (two to six issues), or the maxiseries (seven to twelve issues). Frank Miller's *The Dark Knight Returns* (four prestige format issues) is an example of a miniseries; Alan Moore's *The Watchmen* (twelve deluxe format issues) is an example of a maxiseries.

DIGEST A 4¾″ by 6⅝″ paperback edition. Many of the Archie Comics titles are printed in this format.

MAGAZINE-SIZE 8½″ by 11″, usually a black-and-white reprint of standard format comic book material. *The Punisher* and *Conan Saga* are in this format.

PRESTIGE FORMAT A self-contained story on higher-quality paper and a glossy-cover card stock. A trademark of DC Comics, prestige format is the equivalent of the standard-size graphic novels on the market.

NEW/DELUXE FORMAT Also trademarks of DC Comics utilized mainly for monthly marketing of titles to direct sales. Slightly more expensive, these are made better, and stay in good shape longer than standard-format books. *The Green Arrow* and *The Swamp Thing* are examples of these formats. Marvel also releases books similar to these formats through direct channels.

SUGGESTED FOR MATURE READERS Another direct-sales format used by DC to release comics geared for adults. Since it is intended for sale only to those age eighteen or older, it is free of the jurisdiction of the restrictive Comics Code Authority. Excessively violent comics and those with mature themes and slight profanity usually fall under this format. Books from DC Comics' horror line (*Hellblazer, Swamp Thing,* and *The Sandman*) are examples of this format.

TRADE PAPERBACK A soft-back, perfect-bound, stiff-covered collection or anthology of reprints. *Daredevil: Born Again* and *The Greatest Joker Stories Ever Told* are examples of books currently being reprinted in this format.

GRAPHIC NOVEL Self-contained stories, usually in an oversize format, presented in either hardcover or paperback. DC's *Arkham Asylum* and Marvel's *The Prize* are both examples of a graphic novel.

DIRECT SALES

Direct sales revolutionized the comic book industry in the early 1980s. It created a path for the rise of independent comic companies that had until then been failing because of both a lack of profit and an inability to keep from being lost in the shuffle of the distribution system. Independent companies (known as "Indies"), traditionally low money-makers, were, until the advent of direct sales, faced with giving 20 percent of the cover price of each book to a wholesaler, followed by the distributor, and then the retailer. The new system called for payment to be made up front to the comic book companies, with no returns. Also, by making store owners order only what they could use, the system ended the tendency to have unreasonable print runs and gave birth to the back issues market. Not only were the independent companies given a chance to survive, but the large companies were given the means to save some of their more esoteric titles.

Direct sales also made comic book specialty stores possible. These stores treat collectors as customers—not weirdos or outcasts.

TERMINOLOGY

ANTHOLOGY A collection of stories housed in one issue.

ADAPTATION Material from other mediums (film, literature, etc.) turned into a comic book.

B&W Black-and-white art rather than the usual four-color process used for comics.

COLLECTIBLES Comic book merchandise with the potential to increase in value.

THE COMIC CODES AUTHORITY A strict set of self-policing guidelines instituted by the comic book industry in light of the 1954 Senate Judiciary Subcommittee investigation of the industry.

CONVENTION A public gathering of fans, dealers, and professionals.

CROSSOVER A story line that passes between two or more titles.

DEALER The retailer or liaison to the public.

DEBUT The first appearance of a character, writer, or artist.

DIRECT SALES A distribution system in which distributors buy comics directly from the comic book company, bypassing the traditional wholesale/newsstand distribution process.

FANDOM The inner world or subculture of comic book collectors and fans.

FANZINE A fan publication put out by amateurs.

FORMATS The different designs, styles, or types of comic books.

GENRE A class or category of comic books with specific topics (i.e., super heroes, horror, western, human interest, romance, etc.).

GOLDEN AGE The first era of comic book production—from the early 1930s through the mid-1950s.

GRADING A process of determining the condition of a comic meant for resale (presented in detail on pages 57 to 64).

INDEPENDENT COMICS Books ("indies") not published by major, newsstand-distributed comic book companies.

INTRODUCTION First appearance, same as debut but pertaining only to a character.

ISSUE Single release of a comic book title.

LOGO The design trademark of a character or comic book company.

THE MAJOR LABELS ("The Big Two"): Marvel Comics and DC Comics.

MUTANT A human being with deviating features that make him or her an outcast.

ORIGIN The creation of a character or explanation of how the character came to don its trademark persona.

PANELOLOGIST Slick term for a comic book collector.

PRICE GUIDE A trade publication that helps determine the standard market price for individual comics.

PROMOTIONAL ITEMS Usually posters or T-shirts meant only for the specialty shops and their proprietors.

RARE Only ten to twenty copies of a given issue estimated or known to exist.

REPRINTS New versions of previously presented material.

RETAILER A dealer. Also the owner or manager of a comic book specialty shop.

SCARCE Only twenty to one hundred copies of a given issue estimated or known to exist.

SEQUENTIAL ART Art that is multipaneled, the new-age term for comic book art.

SILVER AGE The comic book era from the late 1950s to the early 1970s that initiated the rebirth of the super hero.

SPECIALTY OUTLET A shop that specializes in comic books and related merchandise.

TRADE Publication related to the comic book industry.

VERY RARE Only one to ten copies of a given issue known or estimated to exist.

First edition issues of the classic adventures of Marvel Comics' *Incredible Hulk* have become expensive. Marvel, however, has begun issuing these stories in slick, hard cover reprint editions entitled *Marvel Masterworks* at far more reasonable prices.

1936
The first non-reprint, single-theme comic book, *Detective Picture Stories*, appears in December.

1937
Based on the quick success of *Detective Picture Stories*, two more non-reprint books soon appear, *Western Picture Stories* in February and *Detective Comics* in March.

People unfamiliar with the world of comics often have a very distorted idea of what that world is made of. Based on their quick perusals of drugstore comic racks, they think there are only two types of comics: super-hero adventures, and simple humor like that found in the various Archie titles. While the caped crime fighters and goofy-teens-damned-eternally-to-high-school do make up about 60 percent of the comic book market, they are but a few of a multitude of genres—some of which are worthwhile to a collector and some which have no potential value. For those who aren't sure, and even for those who think they know all the genres, here's a breakdown:

Captain America, *the golden age World War II hero recently enjoyed his 50th anniversary. The Jack Kirby tales from the forties and fifties were reprinted and released in leather-bound archive editions.*

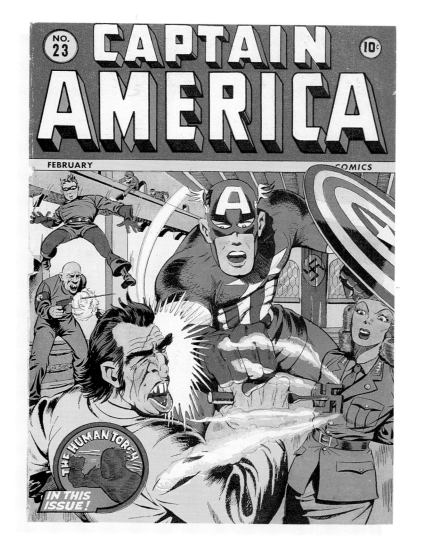

COMIC GENRES 101

SUPER HEROES   This is the land of long underwear, steel fists, and Kryptonite. Despite different innovations from time to time, the theme is generally the same. For the most part, the supermen all forswear killing, and fight for justice day in and day out, and the superwomen maintain tremendous figures and fly into combat in their high heels at a moment's notice.

At present, they are the staple of the comic book industry, especially in America, and are the largest of the many genres. That they are extremely popular cannot be dis-

1938
National Periodical Publications (now referred to as DC Comics, the initials of its own Detective Comics), publishes *Action Comics No. 1* in June. It contains the first appearance of Superman, by writer Jerry Siegel and artist Joe Shuster. Both creators are reported to have been paid around $200 for their work. An immediate success, Superman (who is, when all is said and done, the first costumed super hero) inaugurates the golden age of comic books.

The Avengers *were Marvel Comics'* first super team, featuring the company's best-known heroes. The characters united to battle common foes and raise sales by giving the consumer many heroes in one book. This move is commonly thought to have been in response to DCs' *Justice League Of America in which DCs'* best-known heroes united monthly for much the same purpose.

1939
Detective Comics No. 27 hits the newsstands in May, featuring the first appearance of Batman, created by artist Bob Kane and writer Bill Finger.

puted. They are being transferred to other media more and more. Captain America, Batman, and the Avengers have appeared in novels. Doctor Strange, Wonder Woman, Spider-Man, and The Incredible Hulk have all made it to television with varying degrees of success. Superman and Batman have been the focal points of both hit television shows and movies. Early issues of comic books featuring major super heroes are extremely valuable, and it is nearly impossible for most collectors to obtain original releases. Many times, though, these comic books are reprinted in other formats.

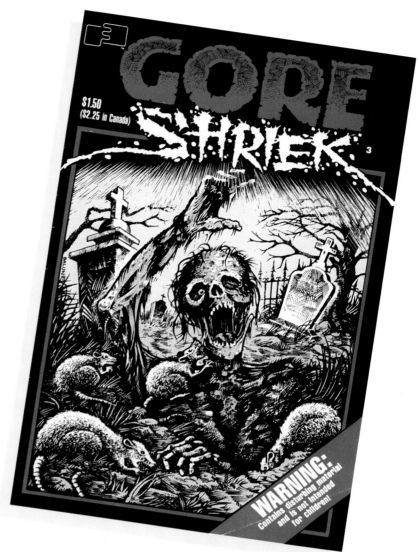

Many independent horror comics today still rely heavily on explicit gore and violence, but the adult-oriented horror line of DC Comics features intelligent, dark, psychological stories. Many collectors feel that DCs' approach is more in line with where the genre is actually heading.

HORROR   Over the past decade, thanks to the popularity of related film and literature, horror has grown more than any genre, enjoying its highest level of success since the early 1950s. The reputation and availability of horror comics was damaged by the institution of the Comics Code Authority in the mid-1950s, when horror comics were confined to a few harmless standard format titles and a group of larger magazine-size format titles.

But in the early 1980s, horror comics rebounded, largely aided by both the advent of direct sales (to escape the Comics Code Authority) and the British invasion

1939
Motion Picture Funnies Weekly, produced to be given away at movie theaters, features the first appearance and origin of the Sub-Mariner, by Bill Everett.

when a number of top British comic book writers and artists came over and injected new blood into American comics. The most successful was *Swamp Thing* written by Alan Moore. The first of the British writers to take the United States by storm, he brought a refreshingly adult, intelligent narrative to the revived title. The early editions of Alan Moore's *Swamp Thing* (he has since left the title) are becoming increasingly valuable.

The second major horror title was *John Constantine: Hellblazer,* a spin-off from *Swamp Thing.* What helps to make both titles popular is the fact that, unlike most horror titles of the past, both of their story lines revolve around a central, continuing character. They both also feature painted covers, rather than the standard four-color ink, making them more attractive to the browsing comic book buyer.

SCIENCE FICTION/FANTASY:

Today science fiction and fantasy remain, sadly, relatively superhero saturated genres with the likes of the Silver Surfer, Thor, and Conan the Barbarian dominating the scene. The British comic anthology *2000 A.D.* has produced a great deal of innovative science fiction with its variety of related characters, such as Strontium Dog (an outcast mutant bounty hunter) and the highly-popular Judge Dredd. France's *Metal Hurlant* revolutionized the science fiction/fantasy genre in Europe and abroad, featuring highly revolutionary art and stories. Those are only two titles, however, in what remains an underutilized field. The latest attempts to make use of the genre have been anthologies such as *Eclipse's Orbit,* adapting stories from *Isaac Asimov's Science Fiction Magazine.* But, adaptations do not a genre make. Unfortunately, although there have been many non-super-hero science fiction/fantasy comics over the years, few non-adaptations have made even the slightest impact in the marketplace.

As in both film and literature, westerns have died as a genre in comic books. Except for a rare miniseries such as Marvel's *Rawhide Kid*, westerns have virtually disappeared from today's comic racks.

WESTERNS

During the 1940s and 1950s westerns enjoyed the height of their popularity, dominating film and television as well as comic books. Today, westerns are an all-but-forgotten medium in a market interested mainly in super heroes and horror. The only westerns selling today are golden age reprints and the *Blueberry* graphic novels. *Blueberry* sells well only because it features the art of Moebius, adding a European flair and dimension to a traditionally American genre. Other than *Blueberry*—potentially valuable because of its art—older western comics are presently valuable only for nostalgic purposes.

1939
In November, the first issue of Marvel Comics published by Timely is released, featuring The Human Torch by Carl Burgos and a colorized reprint of the first Sub-Mariner story.

1939
Will Eisner's *Spirit* makes its first appearance in a Sunday newspaper supplement.

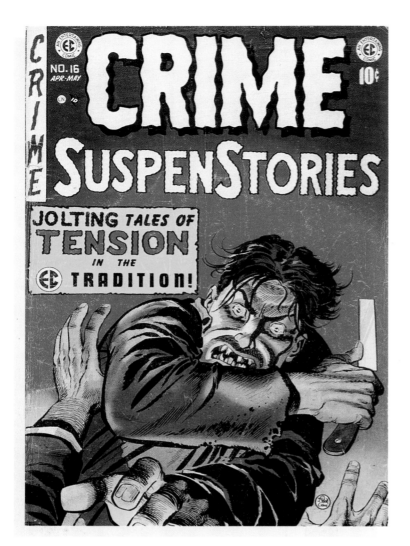

EC's *Crime Suspense Stories* was one of the titles canceled after the institution of the Comics Code Authority. This genre has recently been revived by several independent comic book companies, and is once again growing in popularity.

1940
Detective Comics No. 38, dated April, introduces Robin as Batman's sidekick.

1940
Batman Comics No. 1 is issued by DC Comics; both The Joker and Catwoman are introduced.

MYSTERY/CRIME

Although mystery and crime stories are currently enjoying a renaissance in print, they remain dead genres in comics and are used only in conjunction with super hero, horror, or science fiction titles. Television and the movies have dulled the appeal of four-color police or private eyes. Classic detective, mystery, or crime stories can be obtained through either back issues or reprints of golden and silver age titles; however, most such titles are now running to double and triple digits in price.

MILITARY/WAR/ESPIONAGE

Military or war comic books have been popular through the years as tools of propaganda, glorifying the American cause in various conflicts. Comics such as DC's *Sgt. Rock*, or EC Comics *Frontline Combat* (recently reprinted in a case-bound edition) are good examples of the genre.

Today, the war trend has leaned toward the Vietnam conflict with a variety of titles, including *Semper Fi'* and *The Nam*. *The Nam*, written and created by Vietnam veteran Doug Murray, was all the rage when it was first introduced, but sales have since dropped and early issues that were at one time costly are now reasonably priced and accessible.

Most of the war titles on the market (such as *G.I. Joe*) have evolved into espionage books to remain afloat, but so far none has turned into a major collectible.

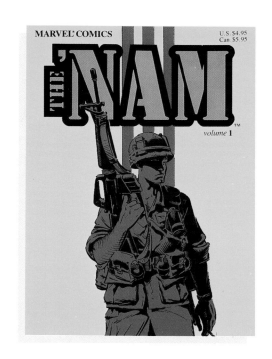

MUSIC
Books devoted to a particular musician or group—almost always presented as a history—are usually just a one-time production. Though the writing and art in these books are usually weak, they do tend to sell out. The first issue of *Rock and Roll Comics*, featuring the group Guns and Roses, quickly disappeared from the stands despite protests from the group that they had not given the publisher permission to produce the book. Subsequent issues featured groups such as Bon Jovi, Whitesnake, Motley Crue, the Rolling Stones, and Kiss. Of course, issues featuring a flash-in-the-pan group could become completely valueless very quickly.

EDUCATIONAL
Educational comics have traditionally been shunned by comic book collectors with the exception of *Classics Illustrated*, the adaptations of classic novels and short stories. Recently revived by First Comics and Berkeley Books, using top names in the fields of comic books, *Classics Illustrated* again is claiming to always faithfully represent the work being adapted. But educators and comic genre critics find them to be mostly a junk product that will never be much of a collectible. Most other educational comics exist in the form of government and corporate handouts. Rarely have any of these held any interest for the average collector.

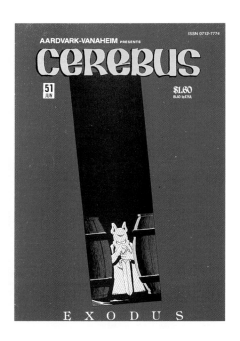

HUMOR

A wide market just beginning to grow again, humor is found in digest form in supermarkets and just about every newsstand that sells comic books. Archie Comics is popularly perceived as being the pinnacle humor line. While it continues to sell well and is constantly copied by dozens of other companies, the Archie Comics line is only one of the many types of humor books found in the marketplace. Satire, bizarre or sick humor, funny animals, and parody are among the many types of humor being published in comics today.

Some books center around a main character or story line (for example, Marvel's *Groo the Wanderer*). Others feature "funny animal" alternative universes such as the various Disney books featuring the likes of Mickey and Minnie Mouse, Donald Duck, and others, or Kevin Eastman and Peter Laird's *Teenage Mutant Ninja Turtles,* a parody of teenage super teams and martial arts adventure. The Turtles have become the biggest merchandising boom of the late 1980s and early 1990s, spawning a variety of related goodies such as cartoons (both broadcast and video), action figures, games, puzzles, hundreds of toys, and a major motion picture. The unfortunate side of this trend is the oversaturation of the market with numerous reprints that makes the Turtle titles mostly worthless to a collector looking to eventually resell the books for a sizable profit.

On the other hand, *Cerebus the Aardvark,* another major "funny animal" title, published by Aardvark Vanaheim Press, is one of the comics credited with pioneering direct sales and independent comic book publishing in North America. At first a "funny animal" parody of Conan the Barbarian and other Sword and Sorcery types, its popularity grew as it evolved into a satirical look at politics and society. Early issues of the title are now valuable and originals are costly or unobtainable for most collectors, though reprints featuring the early story lines are available. (Note: The Turtles have decreased in value over the years since they were only a fad, not a product with substance and durability. Cerebus, on the other hand, a finely crafted satire, has continued to increase in value over the years.)

There have always been a plethora of anthology humor comics such as *MAD, Sick, Beautiful Stories For Ugly Children,* and *Neat Stuff.* Humor seems still to be a good investment since early issues can still be had at near cover prices.

POLITICAL

With the decline of the underground comic movement, political comics have also faded. It is true that such books are still with us—Eclipse's *True War Stories* and *Brought to Light.* D.C.'s *V For Vendetta* and others have also been produced in recent years, but the sad reality, however, is that they have not been well received. Most modern political comics have been nothing more than left-wing kneejerk diatribes, of little interest to comic fans and thus more or less valueless.

ROMANCE

Presently a dead genre in a male-dominated marketplace, romance comics were popular during the golden and early silver ages of comic books. During the late 1940s, Jack Kirby, creator of many of the present-day Marvel comics super heroes, and Joe Simon created *Young Romance* and *Young Love* for Crestwood Comics. After the Comics Code Authority was instituted in the mid-1950s, when most of the popular horror and violent crime comics had to cease publication, romance comics flooded the market only to fade away with the re-emergence of the super hero in the early 1960s. Today, romance is relegated to subplots in super hero titles or sexually explicit comic books, but is no longer a viable market.

SEXUALLY EXPLICIT

Growing out of the ashes of the underground comics are the sexually explicit comics. Titles such as *Black Kiss, Cherry, Omaha The Cat Dancer,* and *Melody* appear in most specialty stores, usually somewhere in the back, sectioned off from the "kiddie" books. These titles run the gamut from mostly

1940
The first continuing funny animal series, *Walt Disney's Comics and Stories,* debuts.

1940
Whiz Comics appears in February and features Captain Marvel, the creation of writer Bill Parker and artist C.C. Beck. Captain Marvel (with the help of writer Otto Binder, who would write the bulk of the material) becomes the only golden-age super hero to surpass Superman in comic book sales.

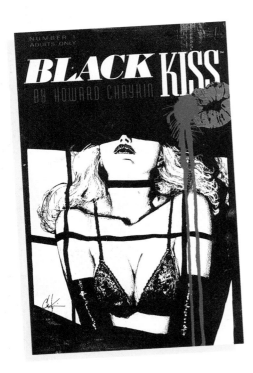

harmless sex fun to hardcore bondage-and-sadism bloodbaths.

Omaha the Cat Dancer, the self-proclaimed "most controversial comic ever published," details the life and loves of a nude feline dancer. It was one of the comic books singled out when a comic book specialty shop named Friendly Frank's was "busted" for selling obscene comic books in December of 1986, bringing new calls for censorship of the comic book industry. Although the conviction was reversed, the charges against Friendly Frank's did not help the reputation of the industry.

Howard Chaykin's *Black Kiss* from Vortex Comics was dropped by Ronald Printing of Canada because of its violent sexual content, despite its being one of the top-selling independents presently on the market. Obviously not for sale to minors, early issues of these comics have become valuable only because of the attention the Friendly Frank's court case garnered, and Chaykin's reputation which has carried over from other projects.

WHO NEEDS SUPER HEROES?

*S*ince the re-emergence of comic books in the early to mid-1980s, super heroes have regained the massive popularity they enjoyed during the golden and silver ages of comics. They have changed, evolved, and matured through the years, but their significance and symbolism remain. The first super heroes emerged on the scene in the 1930s, a time when gangsters ran wild, the police and the government were known to be corrupt, and science was pushing myth and the Bible closer to the dust heap every day. In response to a world too frightening to live in, two teens, Jerry Siegel and Joe Shuster, created the first super hero, Superman. He was better than anyone: brighter, stronger, kinder, and completely incorruptible. Ironically, he was also an alien, originating from the planet Krypton.

The adults in charge of the world's publishing empire turned the project down repeatedly until one with a spot to fill reluctantly took it on. No one but its creators had any real faith in the idea, but reader reaction sold it for them. And, once Superman proved the crying need for tales of a world better than it then was, drugstores were jammed with Superman titles and buyers.

Many of the first comic book super heroes were either detectives in rehashed mystery stories or symbols of American justice and patriotism created in response to Nazi and Japanese aggression during World War II. Big-chinned super guys ruled the comics world for some time after.

Unfortunately, too many of the storytellers did not understand their function and allowed the characters to turn into parodies of themselves (much the same as what has happened to big-screen heroes today).

Stan Lee and Jack Kirby were the first creators to break this trend. To spruce up sales for Marvel Comics in the early 1960s, they introduced characters that were either godlike (Thor) or realistic (Spider-Man, whose alter ego, Peter Parker, was a social outcast). Gone were gangster-type criminals, and in their place came the emergence of the super villain. What made these new heroes so immensely popular was their straightforward earnestness and the average reader's ability to identify with them.

Super heroes are mostly invincible and though a few may sometimes fail in their quests, they are always victorious on some level. They are able to overcome adversity, personal tragedy (for example, the death of Batman's parents), and personal handicaps (such as Daredevil's blindness).

Unlike in the real world, in super hero comic books, justice is always served. The super hero usually achieves this in a few issues with power, speed, and intensity. Super heroes give the reader the ability to transcend his or her world. For the duration of the story the reader gains more strength, power, and fame than he or she will ever have in real life.

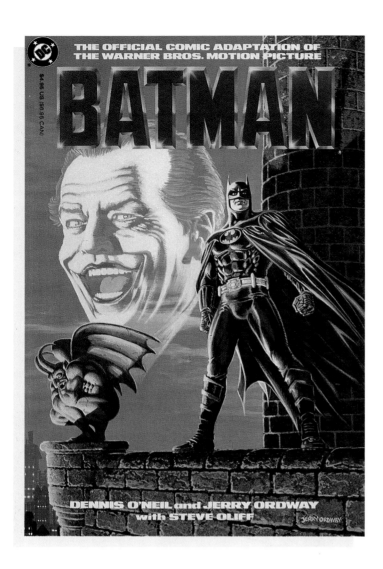

THE OFFICIAL COMIC ADAPTATION OF THE WARNER BROS. MOTION PICTURE

BATMAN

$4.95 US ($6.95 CAN)

DENNIS O'NEIL and JERRY ORDWAY with STEVE OLIFF

Comic book adaptations of other mediums such as Batman: The Movie are usually of interest only to those who enjoyed the film. Generally such merchandise remains valueless to the serious panelologist.

1940
Street and Smith Publications releases *Shadow Comics* in March and *Doc Savage Comics* in May, based on its own extremely popular pulp magazine characters.

1940
Timely Comics (later to become Marvel Comics) introduces Captain America, created by Jack Kirby and Joe Simon.

efore setting goals for a collection, one needs to get a basic feel for what the comic book market has to offer—what is worthwhile for collectors looking to eventually make a profit (what has value, the potential to become valuable, and no potential at all).

Older comics from the golden and silver ages that have completed their runs are often already established as valuable commodities. These will fluctuate or increase in value with age and are only of interest to a collector with available funds looking to make long-term investments.

Older comics whose character(s) survive today in either continuing or revived series fluctuate in price in patterns roughly parallel with their present-day popularity. Obvi-

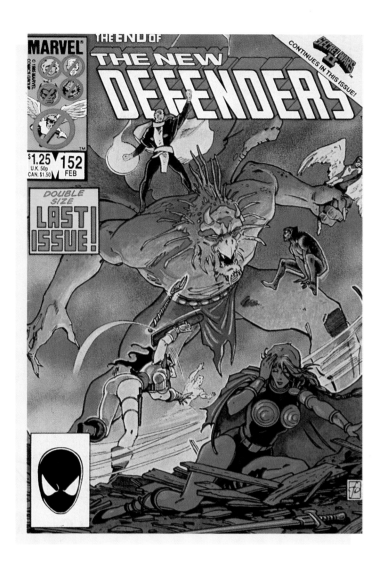

Usually, only comics that have had poor sales announce their final issues, and these are usually of no value to collectors. But, there are exceptions. The final issue of The Defenders *has proven to* be of interest to collectors, because it features Angel and the Beast, current members of the popular mutant title X-Men.

ously, golden-age Detective Comics, featuring the initial adventures of Batman, benefited from the hysteria surrounding the *Batman* movie. The fiftieth anniversary of the creation of Captain America and the surrounding hype caused all of the old Kirby/Simon issues to climb in price.

If you do have the funds to invest in older comics (a near-mint condition copy of *Amazing Fantasy No. 15*, featuring the origin and first appearance of Spider-Man, is valued at an average price of $2,500 [prices vary slightly from price guide to price guide]), then you will have more flexibility to wheel and deal with merchants holding very valuable properties. But for most collectors, especially

1940
The first Superman radio show is broadcast, beginning the crossover of comic book characters to other mediums.

■ *The first printing of a specific title, usually "one-offs" or special releases, are the most valuable to the collector. Each successive printing of a specific release decreases in value accordingly. The number of the printing is usually indicated on the copyright page, though not always. In the case of* Batman: The Killing Joke, *each printing was indicated by the color of the title on the cover (not exactly obvious to the uninformed).*

beginners, large sums of cash are not readily available, so it is more practical to pursue collections of present and recent (ten- to twenty-year-old) releases.

FIRST THINGS FIRST

The most important adjective in a dealer or collector's vocabulary is "first." If it is a first, then it probably has the potential to become valuable. First issues or printings of a comic, regardless of format, are potentially profitable investments. After the first or initial printings of a title are sold out, each subsequent printing's value will decrease by half. Like a horse race, the horse coming in

1940
All-Star Comics No. 3 introduces the Justice Society of America, as the heroes of DC Comics band together for the first time to battle alongside the allied forces during World War II.

An issue which has the death of a major character (which will greatly affect the direction of the title or main character) also has the potential to become valuable. As in the case of ''The Death of Captain Stacey'' in The Amazing Spider-Man, these issues can grow in price to such an outrageous extent that the book can become unobtainable by most collectors (though worthless reprints are usually available).

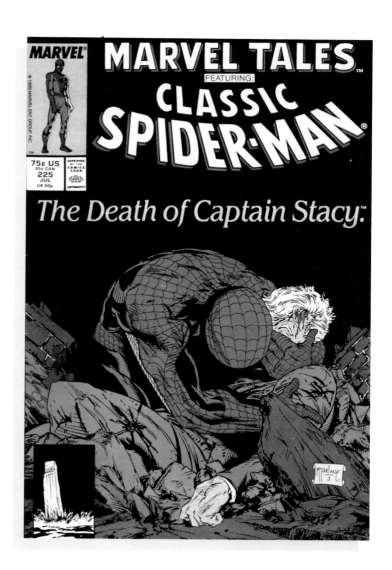

second does not pay nearly as well as the horse coming in first. *Batman: The Killing Joke* in its first printing sells for $20. Its second printing sells for $10. The fourth printing and later printings sell for cover or near cover prices.

You can usually find the number of a book's printing by looking at the copyright page. Some one-shots and special format books will issue different covers with each printing, hoping to attract buyers who will buy multiple copies for cover art; some books, such as *Batman: The Killing Joke*, change the color of the title to signify a difference and change in printing.

First issues of a continuing series or miniseries are also a safe bet. Plucking down change to buy the first issue of

a comic at cover price has made back some smart investments a hundredfold. When a title suddenly gets hot and the back issue prices rise, the first issue price will shoot up quickly, but the prices for the second issue and later will usually rise more slowly. The second issue and later will remain obtainable for some time after, while the first issue will not. The first issue of *The Punisher* (the unlimited, continuing series, cover-dated July 1987) is valued at $8, well over its initial $1 price (an 800 percent increase in just three years).

In this case the character was already collectible, having come off his first extremely successful standard format miniseries (he appeared in solo adventures in two black-and-white magazine-size titles during the mid-1970s), and an outcry for further solo-Punisher material made it a sure bet that the character's first continuing issue would be a successful investment.

The Punisher's above-mentioned miniseries has also become a very valuable property. With the release of the two continuing *Punisher* solo titles (*The Punisher* and *The Punisher War Journal*), as well as his many guest appearances in other Marvel titles, the value of the first issue of the series has jumped from $10 to $23.

First appearances of major characters (both heroes and villains) are also very popular and thus valuable to collectors. Looking at *The Punisher* again, *The Amazing Spider-Man No. 129* containing his first appearance currently sells for nearly $150. In the same vein, the first appearance of a major name's work (writing or art) is considered valuable. The first example of specific writers and artists working together as a team is also sometimes valuable.

The first meetings of two major characters can also be worthwhile to a collector. The two issues of *The Punisher War Journal* where Wolverine and The Punisher first meet have jumped greatly in price despite being only a couple of years old. First-time crossovers or team-ups in titles that normally have only one main character are often profitable. If these crossovers become frequent, however—which often happens if the earlier meeting sold well at the newsstand—successive team-ups will rarely be worth anything.

As detailed in the first chapter, certain formats are sometimes valuable. Specials, annuals, infrequently issued comics or one-shots featuring characters that have their own continuing series or are featured in team books stand a chance of becoming valuable.

The second most important collectible comic next to "firsts" are "major revelations." Any major notation or turning point in a character's continuing story line has the potential to become valuable. The death of a character close to the title hero or of a hero him- or herself or the uncovering of the true identity of a major foe are examples of such revelations. The deaths of Captain George Stacey (in *The Amazing Spider-Man No. 90*) and, later, his daughter, Gwen Stacey (in *The Amazing Spider-Man No. 121*), and the marriage of Peter Parker to Mary Jane Watson (in *The Amazing Spider-Man Annual No. 21*) were all major turning points in the continuing saga of Spider-Man. All these books are worth more than other books from the same time period because of these events.

> **1941**
> *More Fun No. 73*, cover-dated November 1941, marks the first appearances of both Aquaman and Green Arrow.

> **1941**
> *World's Finest Comics* by DC Comics debuts as the first comic book series to feature both Superman and Batman. At first, they appear in separate stories, but by the early 1950s they would begin appearing together, making *World's Finest* the first regular crossover series.

BOOM AND BUST

Another thing to watch for is the latest trend—the way the market is going, what is currently hot, and why. Batmania has given the Midas touch to any related products so far. That will change, however, as the trend dies down. The trick for the collector, of course, is to get in at the beginning of an upward swing of a trend, milk it while it is hot, and then get out again.

Most reprints are usually worthless unless they contain something new for the collector—additional notes from the writer, extra art, a new, hardcover format, for example. Also, it is wise to stay away from most final issues of canceled runs. Unless they have been canceled for special rea-

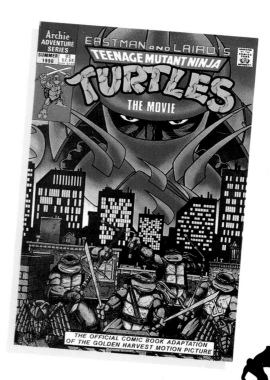

sons—controversy, legal action, stoppage by those who hold the rights to the title character—last issues are worthless. If the canceled character is revived, later issues of a previous run can be had at close to cover prices.

By gaining a sense of what the market is doing—trends, hype, what is going to be released, what is not selling—one learns to make calculated judgments as to what to stay away from and what to go after. However, this basic horse-sense, as it used to be called, comes only after long months, sometimes years, of learning how to wheel and deal. If one is collecting for profit, though, one has to be ready to bargain and take risks, and to swallow some failures. There is no way around it—it comes with the territory.

TURTLEMANIA GOES BELLY-UP

In the mid-1980s, with the release of Mirage's *Teenage Mutant Ninja Turtles,* a black-and-white boom began. When first released, *Teenage Mutant Ninja Turtles* sold more than ten times what the average independent title did.

Inspired by the Turtles' success, numerous new independent companies began entering the marketplace, flooding it with product. Sadly, most of this material was badly written and drawn. It sold, however, because many thought that the limited print quantity of each black-and-white would quickly make them collector's items. The hype helped the fad to grow uncontrolled for more than a year before collectors' hopes of profit faded and they accepted their losses. And, once the market was abandoned by speculators, the black-and-white fad died quickly, since there was little to no real fan interest in most of the comics available.

Dealers and retailers were left with numerous black-and-white titles gathering dust on their racks. Price guides have dropped many of the black-and-white titles from their listings as if they never existed at all.

The 50th anniversary issue of The Flash *took a look at all the heroes who donned the identity of the Flash through the decades.*

t is currently estimated that it would cost more than $700 a month to buy every new comic that hits the stands. And that's not even considering back issues.

Thus comes the first big decision every collector has to make: What does he or she want to get out of a collection? A small, quick profit, a long-term commitment to a full-time business, or a hobby set up purely for fun and personal fulfillment?

Few beginning collectors have the financial resources to collect older titles, at least not at first, so they choose to begin with new books currently on the newsstand. Buying a few titles at a time, ones that look like they're fun

1941
Pep Comics No. 22 appears, featuring the first appearance of Archie, created by Bob Montana.

The classic early adventures of Marvel super heroes, such as The Fantastic Four No. 2 are usually too expensive for collectors trying to build a collection of back issues. Luckily, many of these stories have recently become available in reprint form.

to read, popular ones everyone has heard of, is the best way to find out what is readily available. After a while you can start experimenting, buying titles with which you are only vaguely familiar. In time, you weed out what you don't care for, steering your collection in the most appealing direction.

While many capitalists say "it takes money to make money," this is not necessarily the case for comic book collectors. For mere pocket change, a collector can often make more than 1,000 percent of his initial investment. The only stumbling block is getting in at the start of a trend. It is a good idea to consult one of the trades—*Comic Buyers Guide, Comic Scene*, the *Overstreet Price*

1941
Wonder Woman, created by psychologist William Moulton Marston and artist Harry Peter, appears in the spring issue of *All-Star Comics No. 8.*

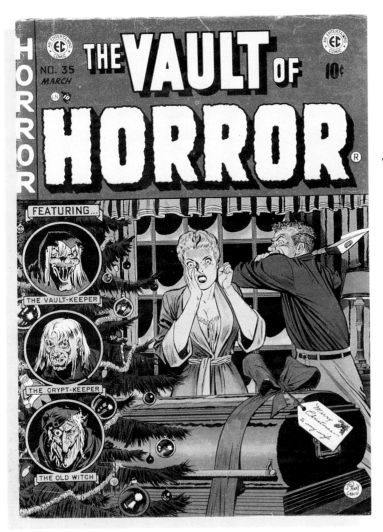

EC horror comics, which have not been produced since the mid-fifties, have become regarded as classics and are now highly priced in their original form. However, Gladstone Publications has reprinted the entire EC horror line for consumption by collectors at news-stand prices.

1941
Jack Cole's Plastic Man and Will Eisner's Spirit are introduced in Police Comics. Charles Cuidera and Will Eisner's Blackhawk is introduced in Military Comics.

Guide, to name a few—as a guide to what to buy for investment purposes.

There are many different ways to collect. Some people like to follow the career of a specific writer or artist; others collect the line of a single company. A fan of horror might wish to collect only horror comics. Someone else might follow each current trend or collect every appearance of a specific character. Whatever the case, what you collect is unique and personal. Even those collecting solely to turn a profit have a variety of choices as to how to go about it.

YOU ARE WHAT YOU COLLECT

The collector should use his or her imagination; ultimately each collection is a reflection of its owner—his or her tastes on display. You should be creative with your collection, remembering that the most important part of maintaining whatever you eventually decide to collect is to have fun. In the end, someone who does not enjoy reading comics will not have a very good collection. Collecting anything without love becomes work, often hard work. And when dealers or specialty store owners notice what to them is a familiar lack of enthusiasm, they will often move in to take advantage of a dissatisfied collector. Anyone who fits this category would find his or her money better invested in penny stock.

When starting a collection, get set up with newer issues first—worry about buying back issues at a later date. Also, it is wise to hold onto books you buy for at least five years before considering resale, unless you are gambling on trends (then just cross your fingers and hope to be able to recognize the right moment to sell). Whatever the case, though, treat collecting as a hobby. Don't demand too much from it, and it will provide great pleasure.

COLLECTING PURELY FOR FUN

Those starting a collection purely for fun (only for personal fulfillment with no intention of resale) have freedoms that the investor/collector does not have at his or her disposal. Whereas an investor/collector must consider resale somewhere down the road, someone who collects purely for fun only has to consider current wants and personal tastes.

Once established at a specialty shop, a collector can inquire about damaged items that cannot be returned to a distributor or publisher. Store owners quickly discover which customers are hard-core collectors and which ones just like to read comics. They will often give a good discount to a "fun only" collector on such items simply because they know he or she is going to keep the book, not offer it for resale.

1945
Max Gaines sells off his super hero properties and begins his own company called Educational Comics (E.C.). The first release is the unsuccessful *Picture Stories from the Bible*.

THE INCREDIBLE HULK Nos. 1-6
by STAN LEE & JACK KIRBY

■ **Marvel Masterworks** *have become very popular among adults who wish to build a library of the comics they grew up with. These books offer silver-age adventures at a reasonable price.*

S ooner or later every collector wants a back issue. The first problems facing the beginner are where to find these issues and how to determine if the price asked is a competitive one.

The number of specialty shops available to each collector will, of course, depend on the size of his or her city or town. Once you have made a store "your" store, you should take the time to go through all the boxes and shelves of comics, examining everything you are thinking about purchasing. If an item is bagged and taped (if it is not, the immediate concern should be for the item's possible degeneration) you should ask the specialty shop proprietor or a salesman to open it. *Never* open a bagged

---

1947
Max Gaines dies in a boating accident and his son, William M. Gaines, inherits the floundering E.C. Comics. He successfully introduces the first crime, love, and western comics.

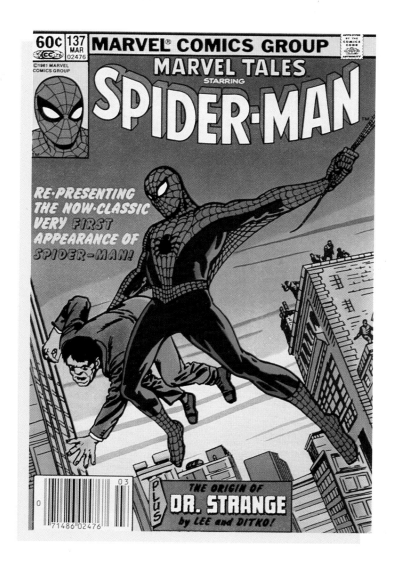

Marvel Tales No. 137 *featured the reprinted first appearance of Spider-Man from Amazing Fantasy No. 15 at a newsstand price. The original printing of AF No. 15 was recently priced at over $2,500.*

comic yourself. Any damage found on a book could be blamed on you. Even if you are not forced to buy it, bad will is no way to start your buying career.

Don't be afraid to comparison shop from store to store. Comic prices often have more to do with individual store owners' ideas on what they can get for something than on any standard pricing system; also, some owners price everything high, expecting the customer to try to talk them down.

Collecting the back issues of popular titles can become costly. If you are collecting for fun, it is always advisable to check on the availability of reprints. The early adventures of *Spider-Man*, for example, very expensive in their

1950
William M. Gaines changes the name of Educational Comics to Entertainment Comics (still called E.C.). He establishes a series of comics known as the "New Trend" with titles such as *Vault of Horror, Tales from the Crypt, Haunt of Fear, Two Fisted Tales, Crime SuspenStories, Weird Science,* and *Weird Fantasy.*

1952
Under the creative direction of Harvey Kurtzman, E.C. publishes MAD Comics (later reformatted as a magazine).

1953
All Fawcett titles featuring Captain Marvel cease publication after years of court litigation in which DC claimed the super hero was an infringement on the copyrighted character of Superman.

1954
In his book, *Seduction of the Innocent,* Fredrick Wertham accuses comics of warping young minds. Following a public outcry, the U.S. Subcommittee on Juvenile Delinquency investigates comic books. In response, major comic book publishers band together and create the Comics Code Authority in October.

original form, are currently available in reasonably-priced hardcover reprints as part of Marvel Comics' "masterworks" series. Later "web-slinger" adventures are currently being reprinted under the title of *Marvel Tales: Featuring Spider-Man.* There is no reason to collect expensive original editions in a personal collection, outside of the desire to own a collection of original editions —a hobby only advised for the rich or shallow.

COLLECTING WITH STAMPS

Mail-order companies found throughout the pages of standard format comic books and the many comic genre trade magazines are good sources for locating and buying back issues. Often an ad will not list all of a retailer's stock. Collectors looking for items should send a query letter detailing their needs along with a self-addressed stamped envelope to several sources at the same time. Mail-order comparison shopping can be time-consuming, but for the collector living in a small town or rural community, it may be the only means of reaching a comics specialty store. Also, prices have been known to vary by hundreds of dollars from company to company on single items. One must remember here that, as with all mail-order establishments, one must be careful when first beginning a new business relationship. There are "rip-off artists" here as in any other marketplace. Asking other collectors who use mail-order companies is the best way to establish the validity of an establishment's reputation. Mail-order companies who operate from specialty shops, and use the mail to attract a national clientele, are usually a safe bet. Also, when starting a relationship with a mail-order company, you should start out by buying a few recent issues for the sake of judgment. If a company guarantees their books are in mint condition but sends damaged goods in the low-ticket categories, you can imagine what it will send when larger sums are at stake.

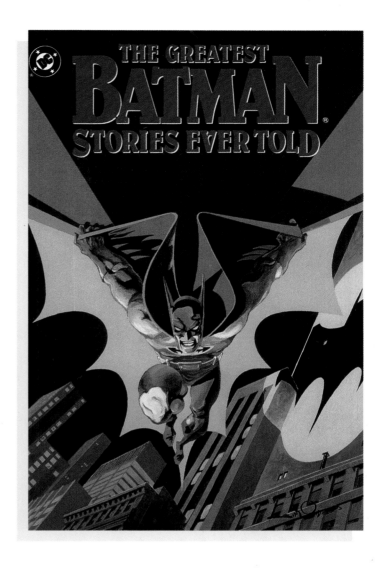

Batman's Greatest Stories *offered a comprehensive look at the evolution of the character since his inception fifty years ago, at a reasonable, trade-paperback price. The original hardcover is more valuable than the more recent trade paperback edition.*

The items that don't move or that are in great demand vary from region to region. Because of this, specialty shops often choose not to carry older, more expensive items that may not move quickly from their crowded shelves. For many collectors, these items can only be obtained through mail-order companies or at comics conventions. Conventions and shows are excellent sources for finding back issues. Many dealers travel the country with these items, specifically gearing their convention sales approach toward their multiregional clientele.

When traditional channels fail, there is the option of placing an advertisement in the classified sections of the various trades. Usually reasonably priced, ads of a few

1955
The impact of the Comics Code Authority forces E.C. to abandon its most popular titles. They launch a new series of titles, all of which are unsuccessful. With issue No. 24, *MAD* changes to a larger magazine format to escape the jurisdiction of the code.

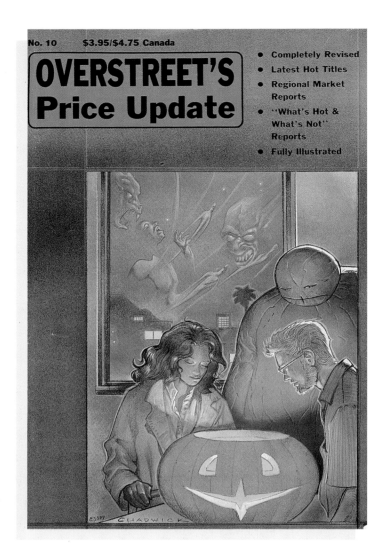

The Overstreet's Price Update, published quarterly to supplement the annual price guide, is one of the best tools of the trade for both the seasoned panelologist and the dealers supplying them.

lines can be placed to attract dealers or other collectors who can fill specific needs. Ads should be precise and short. They should contain only names and addresses— no phone numbers—a post office box is the best address for all such dealings.

Then, once an item is located, the decision must be made as to whether it is worthy of purchase. Once again, don't be afraid to comparison shop; once you see the prices at the various specialty shops you frequent, get estimates from mail-order companies, and then haggle with dealers at conventions.

The price of a back issue is determined by supply, demand, hype, and the price guides. Most price guides are

1956
The silver age of comic book history begins with *Showcase No. 4,* featuring The Flash by Julius Schwartz.

produced on a regular basis—annually with updates, bimonthly, or quarterly, for example—all of them featuring lists of current market prices for comic books of any value. Lists in the various price guides (the best known of which are *Overstreet* and *Comic Buyer's Guide Price Guides*) are said to comprise surveys of recorded convention sales, specialty shops' prices, fanzines' suggested prices, dealers' lists, and the dealings of larger, prominent collectors. But, ultimately, most prices are usually based on the guides themselves. *Overstreet* and other large price guides are fairly complete, listing all titles of any real value. Updates and smaller price guides deal with more current, hot, and, sometimes, ephemeral titles.

The price guide has become the Bible of many comic book collectors, acting as an impartial springboard for most of their transactions. Most prices are based on mint to near-mint grades. The true value of a title can be determined by carefully using the standard comic book grading system.

HOW TO PROPERLY GRADE YOUR COMICS

One of the most important parts of becoming a panelologist, or comic book collector, is learning how to properly assess the true value of any comic you are considering for purchase. Sometimes the slightest imperfection can lower the worth of a book by hundreds of dollars. Without learning how comics are graded before you start buying, you risk the chance of being "ripped off," adding comics to your collection that have no value or, at most, a value nothing near the amount you might have paid.

Consider these two scenarios: One, you correctly predicted that a certain title would skyrocket in price—you invested money and bought multiple copies of the book. Never read and properly handled and stored, the copies appear to be in the same pristine mint condition they were the day you bought them. Yet, when you decide to

1956
After a disagreement with publisher Bill Gaines, Harvey Kurtzman leaves *MAD* magazine.

1961
Marvel Comics introduces the Fantastic Four in November, edited by Stan Lee, the first of Marvel's popular titles featuring more contemporary types of super heroes.

1962
Stan Lee introduces The Hulk (in *The Incredible Hulk No. 1*) in May, Thor in *Journey into Mystery No. 83*, Spider-Man in *Amazing Fantasy No. 15*, both in August, and Iron Man in *Tales of Suspense No. 39*. Marvel Comics would cancel The Hulk's initial run after six issues in March 1963 only to successfully revive the character a few years later as a co-feature with Giant-Man in *Tales to Astonish*.

Properly kept, mint-condition comics, such as the classic **Dick Tracy Comics Monthly** *by Chester Gould,* will be highly graded and offer a good return.

> **1963**
> In July, Steve Ditko and Stan Lee introduce Doctor Strange in *Strange Tales No. 110.*

sell, you are shown that your books are not in mint condition. A dealer, quite happy to list the problems with your copies, tells you that you are not entitled to nearly as much as you had thought. Two, while searching at a convention or specialty shop, you find an issue you need for your collection. You pay what you feel is a good price but upon further inspection in the confines of your home you discover that the book is not worth what you paid.

What can you do to guard against these all-too-common situations? Learn the comic book grading system so you will be able to thoroughly sight-check any book's condition in a matter of seconds.

The grading system used in the United States is perhaps the most stringent in the world. Trading and selling is a dealer's livelihood; they are understandably out to obtain the most profit possible. Arm yourself and be prepared.

MAKING THE GRADE

Grading comics is simple. The following is a breakdown of the standards used to properly grade any comic book (note: Most price guides detail near-mint to good prices, since they tend to lean more toward golden- and silver-age comic books as opposed to newer publications):

PRISTINE MINT
Unlike stamps, coins, and some sports cards, defective comic books are not highly regarded; the better shape a comic is in, the more desirable it is. Period. The highest-quality label a book can receive—*pristine mint*—means the comic is perfect in every way. The cover maintains its original luster and color; all the pages are extra-white and fresh. The spine is tightly bound, flat, and clean. There are no visible marks or blemishes anywhere. The staples have been properly placed; all corners and edges are flat. The trim and margins are properly cut, leaving the front and back covers and all artwork properly centered. It has been printed properly. A pristine comic, showing no faults or imperfections of any kind, can fetch upwards of 140 to 150 percent of the base market price for the same issue in near-mint condition. A comic must be deemed *truly* perfect to be graded pristine-mint, a rare occurrence in standard-format publications, the format under which most mainstream comic books fall.

MINT
Similar to pristine mint, a *mint* comic book is like new or just-newsstand-bought. The cover must retain its full color and luster, while its pages remain white to extra-white. Any flaws, such as spots of missing color at a staple, corner, or edge must be noticeable only upon close inspection. A mint comic book can fetch up to 120 percent of the base near-mint market price.

1963
The X-Men, with art by Jack Kirby, begins in November, but the title impresses nobody. The X-Men lapses into continual reprint after a handful of years and does not enjoy its height of success until its revival during the 1980s.

1965
James Warren introduces *Creepy*, a magazine-size black-and-white comic book, outside the Comic Code Authority's control, featuring some of E.C.'s best writers and artists.

1965
In trying to establish a new satire magazine, Harvey Kurtzman issues *Help*, which, although unsuccessful, features the first professionally published work of Robert Crumb.

Comics that contain only the minor flaws that come from being read a few times, but where the cover retains most of its original color and luster, as in this prime example of C. J. Henderson's and Kevin Farrell's *Ninja*, will usually be graded as *very fine*.

1966
ABC broadcasts the first episode of the Batman T.V. series, with Adam West as The Caped Crusader. While the show quickly creates one of the hottest fads of the 1960s, it would soon leave many people with a bad taste in their mouths about comics. They couldn't take them seriously anymore.

NEAR MINT   Almost flawless, tightly bound, flat, and clean, a *near-mint* comic book has just enough minor defects or wear to keep it from being deemed mint. Any noticeable defects should be minor and would be attributed to the production process, that is, printing, cutting, folding, stapling, shipping. Its cover has lost only minimal luster and color. The pages must be creamy to white in color (though slight discoloration can be allowed in *older* comics as a sign of aging).

VERY FINE   A *very fine* comic can contain some slight signs of wear—wrinkles or minor creases, the effects of having been read several times. Without the flaws created by being handled and read, this comic book would otherwise be classified as either near-mint or mint (this is why it is important to carefully handle the books in your collection). The book is flat and clean. The cover retains most of its original printing color and luster. All pages are creamy to white in color, though a slight yellowing is acceptable. A very-fine book will get between 75 and 80 percent of the near-mint market price.

FINE Tightly bound with slight noticeable wear, a *fine* comic book is still flat, clean, and shiny. While more creases and stress lines are acceptable than in a very-fine comic book, there can be no writing on the cover, tape repairs, or dark yellowing of the pages. A fine comic will still catch the panelologist's eye with a pleasant appearance and will command 60 to 70 percent of the asking price for the book in near-mint condition.

VERY GOOD Showing signs that it has obviously been read many times, a *very good* comic's cover has lost most of its original luster. The cover and pages may show signs of discoloring. There are signs of wear and perhaps some minor markings, but none that might deface or severely soil its cover or pages. It may need slight repair along its spine, and the centerfold may be loose. The cover might have a minor tear, a corner might be dog-eared or folded, and slight yellowing of the pages is acceptable. Older books such as golden- and silver-age comics are often marketed in this condition. Very good books will receive around 40 percent of the near-mint market price.

GOOD A *good* comic book is an average, used-looking copy that still has both covers and no missing panels. While it may be soiled, slightly torn, or have a rolled spine, it still remains sound and complete. Very worn, a good comic may contain minor tape repairs, though this can be deemed as an additional defect, dimin-

1967
Zap No. 1, by Robert Crumb, becomes the first popular underground comic.

1968
DC Comics revitalizes its line with realistic writing and artwork, specifically, Batman and the Green Arrow by Denny O'Neil and Neil Adams.

1970
Marvel Comics introduces *Conan the Barbarian* (based on the fiction of Robert E. Howard, edited by Roy Thomas, with art by Barry Windsor Smith) to the world's comic readers. It enjoys huge success.

ishing the price (about 20 percent of the near-mint price) accordingly. A slight browning of the pages, but no brittleness, is sometimes acceptable in older comics.

FAIR: Heavily read and soiled but complete, with the possible exception of a larger tear in the cover, a *fair* comic book is usually extensively damaged. Even if it needs significant repairs, however, it must remain complete and legible. A fair comic book will usually bring in about 10 percent of the near-mint asking price.

COVERLESS BOOKS: *Coverless books* are almost always worthless. Color photocopied covers may increase salability, and high-demand books can sometimes get up to 30 percent of the asking price for a comic in good condition. Coverless books are ideal for those who are collecting for fun, since they make otherwise unobtainable golden-age and silver-age books accessible at a reasonable price.

POOR: Damaged, heavily weathered, or soiled, a *poor* comic book is usually unsuited for profitable collecting purposes, though it may be worthwhile to those who are collecting for fun, since some comics in this condition retain readable stories at reasonable prices.

Age is not a factor in grading a comic book. A brand new comic book should be graded with the same criteria as a silver- or golden-age comic book.

Upon grading your own collection, include all defects of the issues you wish to sell on a detailed list. You should present this list to the dealer you are doing business with or use it as a query to mail-order companies.

Some of the newer comic book formats utilize more durable covers, paper, and inks, so you will be seeing more pristine and mint books as time goes by. Also, because of direct sales many titles will not be as accessible as others, thus increasing in value as they become rare.

Marvel Spotlight: The Son Of Satan *is an example of how a comic from the mid-seventies can age and deteriorate through both little care and repeated use. As shown, it would be graded from fair to good at best.*

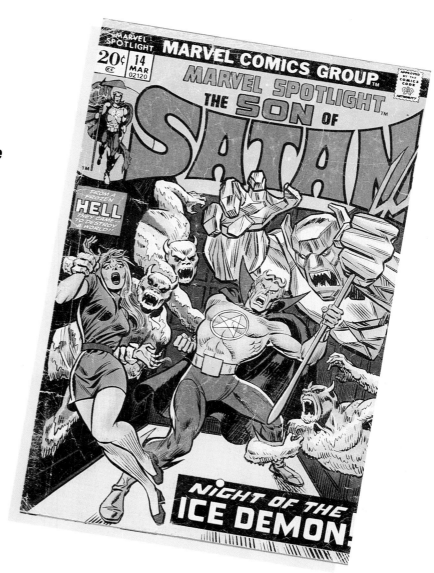

A trend to keep in mind both for one's own use and because of its effect on the market is upgrading. Many collectors buy better-condition issues of titles they already own, then sell off the "lesser" copies they replace. Thus, the informed collector/investor can get the best copies available before the already steep prices climb any higher.

The major disadvantage caused by upgrading is that as the number of lesser-condition copies of a certain title grows in the market and the number of near-mint to pristine-mint copies of the same title diminish, the price percentage as detailed in the preceding breakdown will decrease.

1972
In protest of the Ralph Bakshi's X-rated animated movie, *Fritz The Cat*, creator Robert Crumb skewers the title character with an ice pick in his next comic strip.

If you are unsure of how to grade certain issues in your collection, consult with the specialty shop you frequent, or ask an experienced collector with whom you are friendly. Let them show you examples of each classification. Always ask for an expert opinion if you are unsure of how to grade certain books. While you may find the grading system complex at first, with time and energy, it will eventually become second nature and help you get the most value and enjoyment out of your comic book collection.

SCHMOOZING

Seasoned collectors and readers frequent their shops on the day of new arrivals, or on weekends. If the distributor arrives late, many will wait, standing around conversing. Don't be afraid to get into a conversation; it is a good way of establishing contacts and learning the market. You should learn the names of those you talk with and offer your own; the regulars you establish contact with will help you start a relationship with the owner and proprietor.

Once a rapport with store owners and managers is cemented, the inner portions of comic book fandom will be opened up and special collectible items and limited-run publications will be made available (posters, autographed publications, T-shirts, special orders, unannounced visits by artists and writers, and so on).

New stores are the easiest place to make contacts. Owners and proprietors of new establishments are eager to make friends and gain regulars. Often they will give big discounts, hoping customers will tell friends about their discovery. Whichever way it works, however, your relationship with a comic specialty shop is like any other—the harder you work at it, the better it becomes.

JOIN A CONGREGATION

The comic book specialty shop has become a place of worship, a weekly gathering place for those sharing the same faith. And, luckily, finding a safe house in one of these shops is usually quite easy.

First, locate all the specialty shops within traveling distance from your home or job and then visit each of them. Which ones have the most to offer? Comic shops all have their own atmosphere. It will not take long for you to discover where you feel the most comfortable.

Once you choose a store, you should purchase something each time you visit—don't spend hundreds each time, one comic is fine. It is good to visit the store at least twice a week at first, on the day or the day after the new arrivals hit the stands (usually Thursday or Friday) and during the store's slow period, usually the beginning of the week (Monday or Tuesday). Talk to the owner as you shop. Ask what titles have arrived, what he or she thinks is good, what is coming out later in the year. Any dialogue at all works to establish a relationship. After a while, you will get noticed.

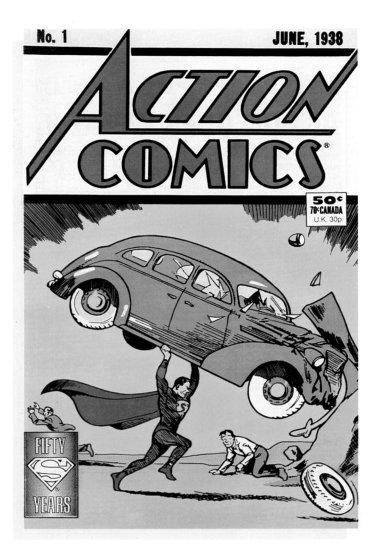
No. 1   JUNE, 1938

ACTION COMICS

50¢
70¢ CANADA
U.K. 30p

FIFTY SUPERMAN YEARS

All early issues of Action Comics featuring Superman have become valuable and thus lucrative to the older collectors who have held onto their issues.

1972
DC Comics' *The Swamp Thing*, created by Len Wein and Berni Wrightson, begins in November, introducing a new era in horror comics.

onsidering the volume and variety of comic books produced over the decades, very few will become extremely valuable like *Action Comics No. 1*, which has been priced at $30,000 for a near-mint copy. Most will barely rise above their cover price. Sometimes a one-shot title like *Teenage Mutant Ninja Turtles* comes along, introduced to the market without fanfare only to rocket into a multimillion dollar business *(Teenage Mutant Ninja Turtles No. 1*, was recently priced at $200 for a first printing). The question: How can a collector predict what title will become hot and valuable—*what* will become the next trend?

It is obviously impossible to clearly predict what is going to turn into the next major trend. There are always

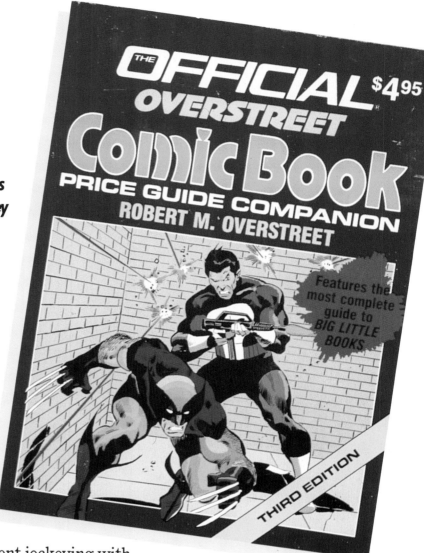

The Official Overstreet Comic Book Price Guide *is the Bible for panel-ologists. All new collectors should use it as the basis for all the selling and buying they plan to do.*

several publications at any given moment jockeying with each other to catch the public's eye. Any one of them can suddenly become just what everyone believes they have been looking for. The best anyone can do is keep up with related news in the trades (especially the weekly *Comic Buyers Guide*), listen closely to specialty shop talk, and follow any growing hype. But the only real way to strengthen your instincts is by studying previous trends.

1973
DC Comics revives the original Captain Marvel in *Shazam*, with new art by C.C. Beck in February.

KEEP YOUR EYES OPEN

Watching what the other media (non-genre magazines, television, film, radio) are up to is often the key to profit-ability. The early 1980s saw the rise of the vigilante in

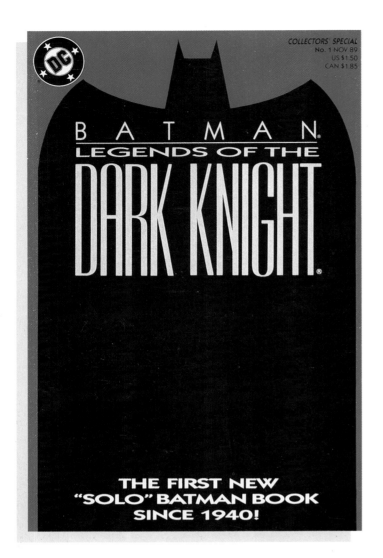

Issue one of Batman: Legends of the Dark Knight *featured five different colored ''false'' covers (a second ''true'' cover was underneath). It was hoped that collectors would purchase multiple copies. The ploy did not work and many shops are now offering the issue at a discount price.*

1973
The Shadow is revived in October at DC Comics by writer Danny O'Neil and artist Mike Kaluta.

film *(Rambo),* pulp novels *(The Executioner),* and the media (Bernhard Goetz). It was only natural that this popularity would translate over into comics. The Punisher, a character who attracted little attention after his creation during the mid-1970s, has become one of the top-selling heroes in the Marvel Universe, starring in two solo titles as well as making numerous special appearances. Likewise, the most famous of all the comic book vigilantes, Batman, would never have made it to the theaters without the same trend. The pivotal Batman story, *The Dark Knight Returns,* by Frank Miller was written as social commentary on the wave of vigilantism. When it turned into a major sensation, the trend grew further, as would

Batmania. For those who were quick enough to buy the first printing of *The Dark Knight Returns* (especially in quantity), the payoff was lucrative.

The X-Men, a poor seller when originally published in the early 1960s, rocketed to the top of the Marvel Comics line in the early 1980s, as it symbolized a team of misfit youths struggling against the norm, something all comic fans could identify with. It also dealt with racism and persecution. As its massive popularity grew, Marvel capitalized by spinning off other titles from it *(The New Mutants, X-Factor, Alpha-Flight,* and *Excalibur).* The most popular of the mutants, Wolverine, would star in his own title, and after gracing the cover of the biweekly anthology series, *Marvel Comics Presents* best-selling issue, he would become a regular in its pages. Mutant titles are currently taking up the better part of Marvel's top ten list and are rumored to sell more than a million copies monthly.

A Death in the Family was the miniseries within a series that detailed the death of the second Robin in the pages of *Batman.* The series quickly jumped from its cover price to nearly $100 for the four-issue set. As the hype and media attention grew, the value of the series rose even higher, and peaked at over $150. As the attention died down and another Robin was introduced, the price quickly dropped. Some dealers who failed to notice when the trend peaked have sold off their excess stock for near cover price.

The trick to making a profit from a trend is to get in at the bottom and sell off your collection as soon as the trend peaks.

Once a postage stamp becomes valuable, in almost all cases it will remain that way; any further movement of its price is usually upward. Investing in postage stamps usually guarantees a profit, never a loss, to the collector.

Sports cards fluctuate based on the career of a given player. Depending on the career of a player, cards issued featuring the player will become valuable (the rookie card or first card issued featuring the player is always the most valuable). If a player's statistics or output should decline drastically during his career, his cards may drop in price. The 1983 Topps update rookie card of Dwight Gooden, a pitcher for the New York Mets, was the hottest card on the market after he won the Cy Young Award in 1985. When he faltered two years later because of cocaine abuse and his statistics dropped off drastically, his card's price drop was equally drastic. Still young, with many potentially productive years left, Gooden may regain his all-star status and his cards may once again become valuable.

This kind of dramatic example is a rare exception, however. Usually, once a player's career is complete, the value of the cards issued will stabilize, only gaining in value with time. The same, sadly, is not true of comic books. Comics, like the stock market, are always a gamble.

The early or first issues of titles whose runs have spanned multiple decades are usually valuable. But if the popularity of a character declines, it will affect the price of their early issues. Conversely, if a character grows in popularity in the present, its early issues will also profit (as is the case with the recent trend of Batmania). The difference that must be remembered is that a sports figure's career depends solely on his popularity. However, many other factors enter into determining a comic character's fame. Dozens of comics' fortunes have been drastically changed by the simplest of changes. A new writer, new artists, or new direction for the book can affect prices greatly.

Also, unlike baseball players, who retire after a decade or two of service, canceled titles always have the chance of being revived somewhere down the road. If an early period of comic books (from the golden or silver age) attracts attention, titles released during that time may also garner notice, making them valuable to collectors for "nostalgic" reasons. If comic book companies notice a "stir" in the popularity of a dormant title they may revive it (such as the recent new runs of *Hawkman, Doc Savage, Aquaman, Deadman, The Shadow, The Sub-Mariner,* and many others). The once stable prices of old comics will rely on the popularity of the new run. Comic book characters are immortal. They never die and always have the chance of resurfacing.

But, while comic book prices are not nearly as stable as postage stamps or baseball cards, the excitement of trying to predict what will become or stay valuable is what makes collecting them so much fun.

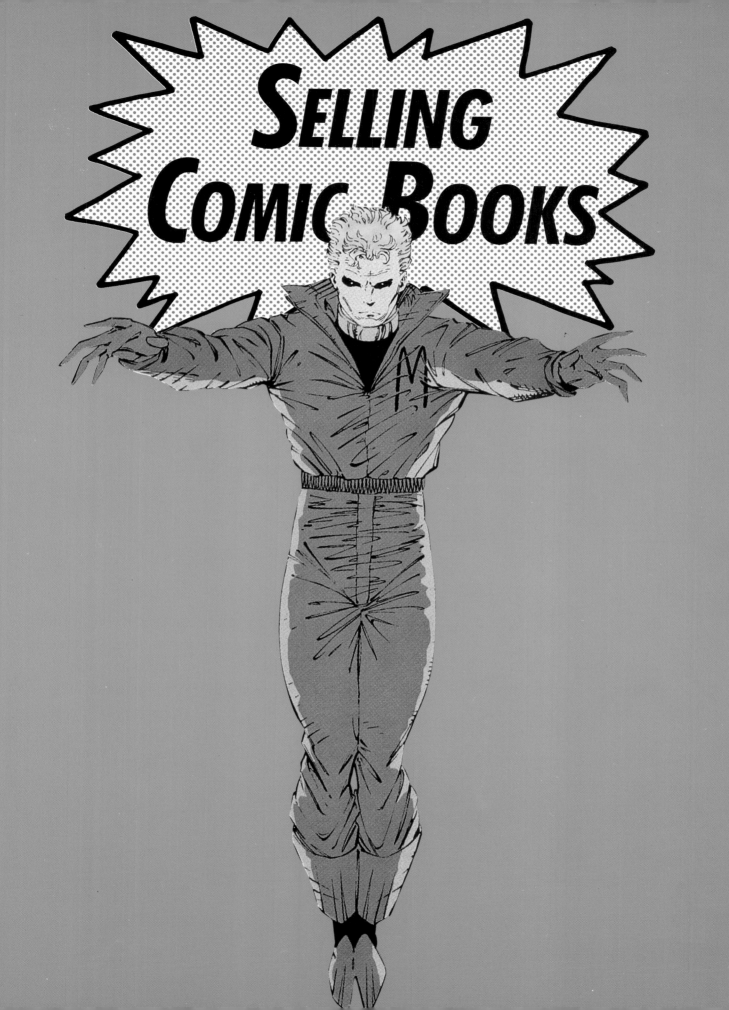

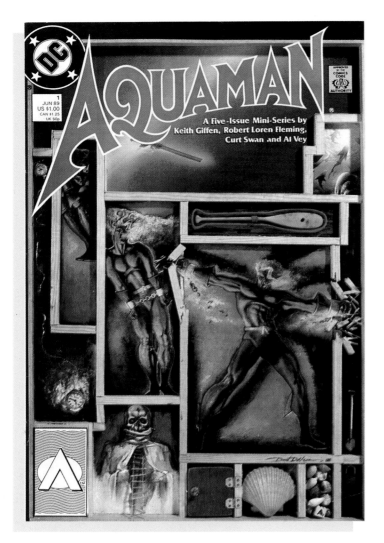

After losing popularity over the past decade, Aquaman was recently featured in a well-received mini-series which has started talk of a new continuing series.

1974

DC Comics reprints classic comic books in an oversize format under the title *Famous First Editions*. Among the books reprinted are *Action Comic No. 1*, *Sensation Comics No. 1*, *Whiz Comics No. 1*, *Wonder Woman No. 1*, *Batman No. 1*, *All Star Comics No. 3*, *Flash Comics No. 1*, and *Detective Comics No. 27*.

When a comic book becomes valuable (a trend has reached its zenith, market hype has caused a demand for the title) and a collector feels it is a good time to sell, he or she must choose between the many avenues available to do so. There is an art to selling comics. If learned and executed properly a collector can get the most for his properties; if not, he or she risks missing out on potential profits.

Where collectors should sell valuable comics depends on the supply and demand of various regions, the monetary threshold of the comic book specialty shops they can reach, the actual value of the title for sale, and other factors. A comic book that may be valuable to one spe-

The first issue of Nth Man: The Ultimate Ninja *has remained relatively valueless since its release last year. There is the possibility that critical acclaim may cause its price to rise. Such acclaim, however, does not seem to be on the near horizon.*

cialty shop dealer may be worthless to a dealer in another part of the country. This is why studying the trades and various price guides is a good idea. Look through the advertisements in these books (as well as those in most standard format comics) and compare their prices for the same items. Most dealers of mail-order companies charging a high price for an item do so because their supply is low and the demand is high. When this is the case, the collector should make inquiries for quotes while comparison shopping. Phone quotes are good if the dealers are within a reasonable distance, though most dealers will not talk money until they see the items first-hand. Query letters, listings of what a collector wants to sell, and a

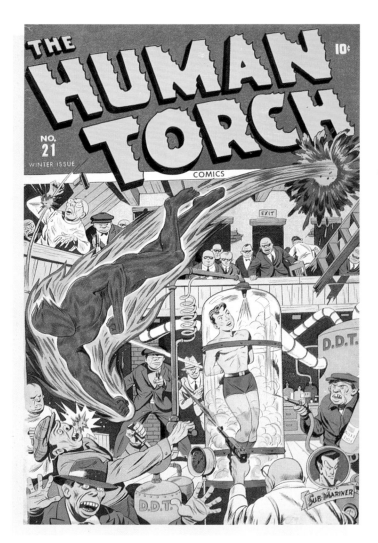

 A golden age issue of The Human Torch *is a good example of what most dealers are looking for in the way of pre-1970 merchandise. Most dealers are willing to bend over backwards to get pre-1970 issues.*

self-addressed stamped envelope for a reply are necessary to begin any initial transactions.

It is important to note that most mail-order companies will not deal with new customers unless the collectors have references to back them up. These references must come from reputable collectors or store dealers (thus making contacts and business relationships necessary). The same works in reverse. It is a good idea to get the opinion of various collectors who have used a particular mail-order house before doing business with it.

Currently, the majority of existing collections are made up of DC, Marvel, and independent comics from the year 1975 to the present. Mail-order companies are mostly

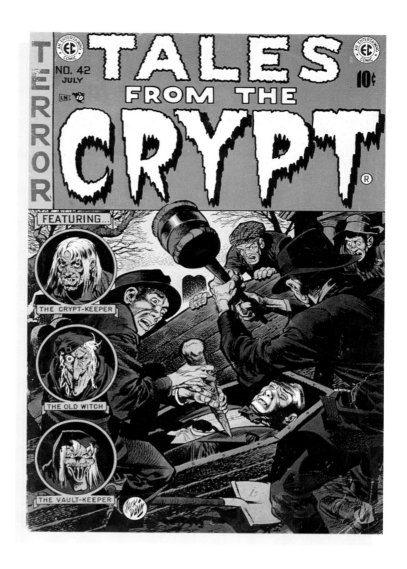

Most mail-order houses prefer to deal in material such as the vintage Tales From The Crypt, *due to its high collectibility.*

interested in titles issued before 1970. Collectors should check the various advertisements available for details as to what the companies are looking for. While many collectors might want to sell their entire collections in one shot, this seldom happens, since dealers do not want to purchase "junk" titles to get at valuable items. A dealer forced to take valueless items will often offer less for an entire collection than he might have for those prime comics he really wanted had they been singled out and haggled over individually.

It is recommended that if the price given for a title a collector is trying to sell is standard throughout most of the country, the collector try to deal it locally, if possible,

1974
The Punisher, based loosely on the pulp novel series *The Executioner* by Don Pendelton, makes his first appearance in the *Amazing Spider-Man No. 129.* Though his solo adventures in various magazine-size Marvel Comics would fail, he would become one of Marvel's biggest titles in the late 1980s.

Wolverine makes his first appearances in *The Incredible Hulk* Nos. *180* and *181*. Created by Len Wein, Wolverine later becomes one of the most popular characters in the Marvel Universe.

Mid '70s
Comic books with titles such as *Akira* and *Lone Wolf & Cub* help make comic books the top-grossing form of adult entertainment in Japan.

1975
Metal Hurlant, a European comic magazine featuring the early work of the French sequential artist Moebius, is released. It later becomes one of the most revolutionary influences on American comics since the underground movement of the late 1960s. Unfortunately it would fold at the end of the 1980s.

at the specialty shop where the collector conducts most of his or her business. A collector will usually get the best price that dealer can offer.

HONESTY IS THE BEST POLICY

It is sometimes a good idea for a collector to pose as a customer and call his or her local specialty shops to inquire about the availability of the titles he or she wishes to sell. This may create a false demand for the title, causing the dealer to make an offer for a product he otherwise might not have purchased. This is not a very subtle trick, however, and will not work more than once or twice before the targeted store catches on to it. Considering the importance of customer-dealer relationship to the customer, capitalizing on such false impressions is not recommended.

When selling, you should go to your local specialty shops and check to see if the titles you wish to sell are openly available, stocked in great numbers on shelves, racks, or in cases. If they are, and they are priced below the average guide listing, chances are the dealer will not want more copies of them.

If a collector does not see the titles in question, or there are just a few copies priced over the average price guide listings, the collector should approach the dealer about what he or she has to sell. Collectors should keep in mind, however, that more valuable titles are often kept behind the counter or in storage rooms and only brought out when asked for.

Advertisements placed in trades or fanzines detailing what a collector has to offer are good ways of bypassing mail-order, convention, and specialty shop dealers. By placing these advertisements, usually for a reasonable rate each month, the collector in a sense becomes the dealer. If one plans to continue such an operation over a long period, it is wise to rent a post office box to conduct

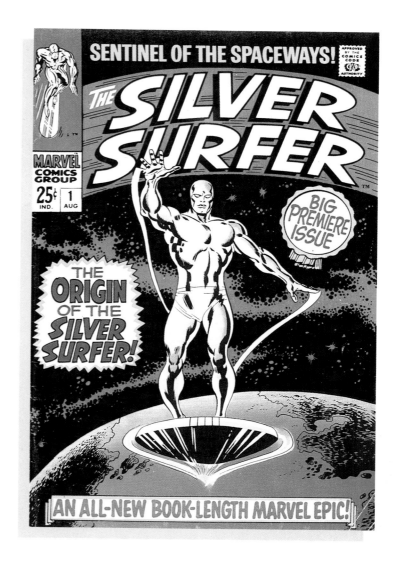

This classic first issue of The Silver Surfer from Marvel Comics, featuring his origin, went up in value recently when the character was again given his own continuing series.

business, since a collector will be dealing with a faceless, anonymous clientele. With time and patience, a collector will eventually get a reaction, and the odds of being successful in this format are fairly good.

In addition to genre-related trades there are computer networks available for collectors to track down as well as sell comics, and get up-to-the-minute news on professional happenings and information on changes in the market. Collectors who own computers with modems should consult the trades or dealers for availability, access, and cost of getting hooked up to at least one of these networks.

Conventions are another good place to sell comic books.

1975
Marvel and DC Comics collaborate on an oversize comic book version of MGM's *Wizard of Oz*.

Dealers who travel the country from show to show will have unique needs since they cater to a multiregional clientele and usually deal in older comics.

Be warned, though, dealers who travel the convention circuit are seasoned hagglers. They are very sharp when it comes to talking dollars. Remember, this is their livelihood. Beginning collectors trying to get the most out of their hobby may find themselves in over their heads. While some may find haggling to be tension-filled hard work, there is an art to it that can help the investor/collector when selling items from his or her collection.

THE ART OF HAGGLING

Most dealers base the amount of money they are willing to spend for back issues on a number of factors—their supply, consumer demand, what money they have to offer, how long they are willing to lock up their investment while waiting to move the title, the rate of business during the given week, their relationship with the collector, and even the mood they are in that day. A collector can use the various price guides for direction as to how much money to ask for, realizing most dealers will offer one-third to one-half of what is listed in the price guides (the dealer must consider the profit that would be made on the sale of the comics).

A collector must always be confident when attempting to sell a property, going into negotiations with the attitude that he or she can always go elsewhere to do business. (Note: In the case of selling to a store where a collector conducts most of his or her business and has developed a standing relationship, stubbornness or arrogance could affect future dealings. This does not mean that you should merely take your local store's best offer every time out of fear of offending the dealer. All a collector who does not like a price has to say is, "Wow; that's all they're worth? Heck, I might as well keep them for now." Then the collector either tries another store or puts the books away to try again six months later.)

A dealer's reaction to what you would like to sell is a pretty good indication of what he or she actually wants and is willing to offer in return. The collector should attempt to get a square price from their dealer up front. This rarely happens, since the dealer most likely will want the chance to get the price down below what he or she would be willing to spend. In this case, the collector should ask for about three-quarters of the average price guide line. If the dealer is offended or declines the offer, the collector should again ask for a price. At this point, the dealer will usually offer a price. If not, the collector should lower his or her price to the lowest amount he or she is willing to accept. If the dealer tries asking for even less, the collector should be polite, say a thanks-but-no-thanks, and take his or her business elsewhere. If the dealer wants the collector's property badly enough the dealer will try to reach a compromise. This especially holds true for conventions where dozens of dealers are competing for every available dollar side-by-side.

CASH OR TRADE

When selling properties, a collector should take personal needs into consideration in determining how to receive his or her just returns. If you need the money you should take it, but it is usually best to take at least a portion of the sale in trade. Most dealers will offer more in trade than in cash, often double the amount. This is especially true when they are buying either very expensive single issues or large quantities of books, which call for larger cash reserves than they have available to make the purchase.

Dealers usually earn one-third to one-half of the cover price of a new title, so they are usually willing to give a little more in trade on new titles since reorder is only a phone call away.

It is important to present each item you wish to sell to

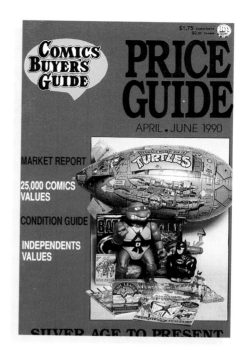

1976
After years of court battles, Jerry Siegel and Joe Shuster are given financial recompense and recognition by DC Comics for their creation of Superman.

Not much can compare to the experience of making a large profit selling comics. Unfortunately, while the comic-trading business can be wildly rewarding, it can also be nerve-racking and frustrating.

Case in point: One collector learned a lesson when he sold a first edition of *The Punisher* limited series. He went to a convention and after a lot of inquiries, found a dealer who was interested. The dealer examined one of the titles for a few moments and then began to point out the many defects he claimed it contained. This aggravated the collector. He had been told when he originally bought the series from another dealer that it was in mint to pristine-mint condition. Yet here was this dealer telling him that the cover wasn't perfectly centered, and its colors were slightly diminished. Still, he accepted the price offered, which was no reward for his time and original investment. All the time the dealer was saying that the titles were hardly worth trying to resell.

Soon, however, a couple of other collectors approached the table asking the dealer if he had the same series the collector had just sold. Acting as if the collector was no longer standing there, the dealer sold the series to the two at more than twice what he had just bought it for, telling the customers the books were in mint condition! He made better than a 300 percent profit for ten minutes of "work." The collector smartened up and no longer feels guilty when haggling. You shouldn't either.

the dealer or potential buyer in a well-kept condition (bagged with a backing board). This helps establish a good first impression and builds a basis for trust.

PRICE GUIDES

The prices listed in the various price guides (*Comics Value Monthly, Overstreet Price Guide, Comic Buyer's Guide Price Guide,* among others) are the average listings comprised of reports from various conventions, fanzines, trades, specialty shop listings, mail-order company listings, and major dealers across the country. These listings, as previously mentioned, should be used as a guide and not as law.

1977
National Lampoon publishes *Heavy Metal*, the first Euro-style American comics magazine based on the French magazine *Metal Hurlant*.

1977
The first Superman film is released. An immediate success, it proves to filmmakers that comic book characters can be lucratively translated to film and television.

One of the keys to predicting trends is understanding hype, the positive attention (necessarily from many different channels) that makes a character, writer, artist, or title hot enough to propel it into a full-blown trend. Understanding hype, however, is to know that it is often a ploy used by merchants to drum up support and attention for a new or slumping product. This is not to say that hype does not sell, just that you shouldn't be fooled by it.

During the early to mid-1960s, many Marvel Comics covers contained statements such as ''the greatest team-up of all time,'' or ''the start of a new era of comics.'' This worked for a few years, keeping Marvel fans entertained

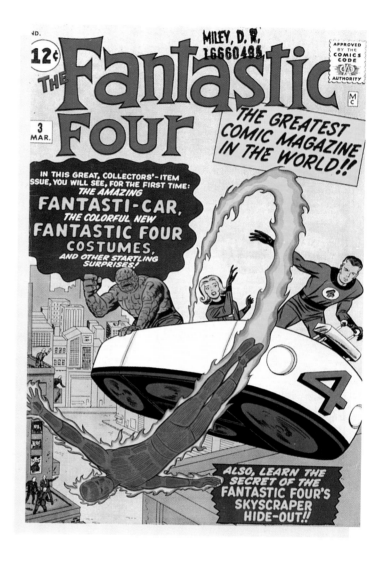

"The greatest comic magazine in the world" is a matter of opinion and should not be decided by a comic book company. Hype like this is overused, and has become meaningless. Don't judge a book by how it promotes itself on its cover.

and enthusiastic. After a while, though, the "pulse-pounding," "biggest," "most spectacular" cover balloons of all time began to grow annoying. In fact, once readers began seeing the words "the greatest adventure ever told —this is the big one" gracing the covers of comics every few months, not only did Marvel begin to lose its credibility with its fans, but its flamboyant self-aggrandizement actually made it the butt of industry jokes for years. (Indeed, never ones to learn a lesson easily, Marvel is risking running their success with "mutant" books into the same hole. So desperate are they to get the M-word on the covers of all their books, they even called Spider Man the "non-mutant superhero" in bold colorful letters.)

1977
2000 A.D., the English based futuristic comic anthology that later introduces Judge Dredd, is released.

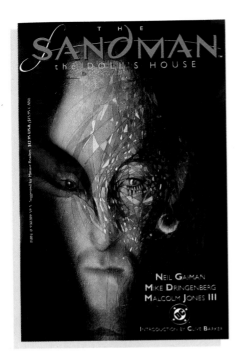

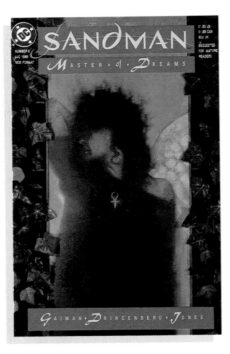

Marvel is not the only guilty party, however. Many other comic publishers still do the same today. And all of them issue promotional fliers and posters and take out full-page advertisements in trade publications pushing their products in the same old way: "An adventure beyond all imagination!" or "The most controversial comic book ever published." The "For mature readers only" angle is just the latest ploy in the hype wars. Shamefully, hardly any comics ever stand up to their prerelease hype.

Don't be fooled by hype. Instead, keep a lookout for other readers' reaction to it. If a title gets hot, get in on it, and sell when the hype begins to wane.

HYPERREALITY

In the months preceding the release of the first issue of *Teenage Mutant Ninja Turtles*, a rumor was spread around the comic book community suggesting that the first release of the run would only be a few thousand copies. This tied in with the publisher's hype that the book was to be a parody of the then current trends in mainstream comics. Dealers, faced with the prospect the book would be a hit, ordered heavily. Collectors scurried about to get multiple copies. Then, insider rumors reported the publisher held back copies on all orders to create the impression that there were so many orders they could only fill half of what they wanted. Whether this is true or not, it is plain to see that the company's hyping of the Turtles created an artificial demand for a book no one knew anything about.

Hype is often created unintentionally by outside elements. DC Comic's *The Sandman* written by Neil Gaiman is perhaps the most intelligently imaginative comic book available today. Unfortunately, due to its lack of sensationalized super heroes and super villains, it never reached the wide scale audience it deserved—not until *Rolling Stone* magazine entered the picture.

In the annual "Hot" issue (dated May 17, 1990) which proclaims what is currently trendy, *Rolling Stone* writer Mikal Gilmore gave praise to *The Sandman* calling it "a powerful new literature, fresh with the resonance of timeless myths." DC Comics, looking to capitalize on this positive attention, accelerated the release of a trade paperback of *The Sandman's* "The Doll's House" storyline without giving any advance notice, a rare marketing move for a comic book company. In their monthly flier "Coming Comics," DC explained they were going to treat the book as an item already in stock rather than accept pre-orders, so the book could be on store shelves as close to the release of the *Rolling Stone* article as possible.

Because they'd been given advance notice that the "Hot" issue article would appear, DC was also able to place a full page advertisement for the trade paperback in the middle of the *Rolling Stone* article. In this case, the excess hype was justified (to bring worthwhile comic book literature to a broader audience), but this is not always the case. A collector should be hesitant to buy into such hype.

Hyping a product is dangerous. Sometimes it hurts a product's image, sometimes the publisher's wallet— sometimes the wallets of the dealers, store owners, and collectors. The only good advice is the old adage: Believe half of what you see, and nothing of what you hear. In fact, in this day and age, it is probably safer to make it a quarter.

1977
Elfquest is released; it is the first of the flood of independently owned and marketed black-and-white comic books, which will be released with increasing regularity over the next decade.

1977
The first issue of *Cerebus the Aardvark*, by Dave Sim, debuts in December. It quickly becomes the most successful independent black-and-white comic book of all time.

1978
Empire, by Samuel R. Delany and Howard Chakin, is the first graphic novel released by a major publisher.

1978
Steve Gerber sues Marvel Comics for the rights to own his creation, *Howard the Duck*.

BATMANIA

The best example of well-orchestrated hype is the anticipation and excitement that surrounded the opening of the 1989 Warner Brothers film, *Batman.* An action-packed movie trailer preceded the film's June 23 release by more than half a year, causing skeptics to take note when film-goers received and applauded it more than the feature presentations with which it was run. The slow-building hype had grown into full-blown hysteria and the results were lucrative for all involved. Of course, this did good things for the price of Batman comics.

Part of the hype for the movie was engendered by the 1986 release by DC Comics of Frank Miller's haunting and apocalyptic *The Dark Knight Returns.* The landmark miniseries depicted Batman as a middle-aged man returning to action after a decade in retirement. This series rocketed Batman books to their highest collectibility in years and set the stage for the film to come. In fact, the 1989 film's atmosphere and set design were taken in great part from Miller's work.

As the popularity of the character grew, media critics began to target Batman as proof that comics had matured. DC Comics was not slow to capitalize on the hype. In 1988, in compliance with reader outcry over their dissatisfaction with the second Robin, Jason Todd, the company orchestrated a phone-in poll to decide the fate of the character. The reaction led to Robin's violent death at the hands of The Joker (though it has been rumored that an ending where the Boy Wonder lived was never even written). DC made sure the story was headline news.

Fueled by hype about who would star in the upcoming movie, Batman dominated the comic book and toy industry in 1989. By the time the film opened in June, Batman had created a merchandising frenzy as well as a fashion. It was impossible to go anywhere without seeing someone wearing a Batman-related item.

Although comic book specialty shops had trouble competing with larger stores, they enjoyed their greatest success since the comic book boom of the early 1980s thanks to Batmania.

The explosion of the character of Batman's popularity in the marketplace made it possible for new high-profile projects to be undertaken that might have been lost, rejected or hidden in low-key, standard-format comics. Among the new items to hit the stands were *Gotham by Gaslight,* a look at the Batman who might have existed during Jack the Ripper's reign of terror; *Arkham Asylum,* an intelligent look at the institution where Batman's insane enemies are sent (the top grossing direct-market-only comic book ever, with advance sales of over $2.5 million); and *Digital Justice,* a completely computer-generated graphic novel.

The death of Batmania finally came during the winter of 1990. The multitude of Batman-related merchandise had finally begun to irritate collectors to the point where they would refuse to buy the items.

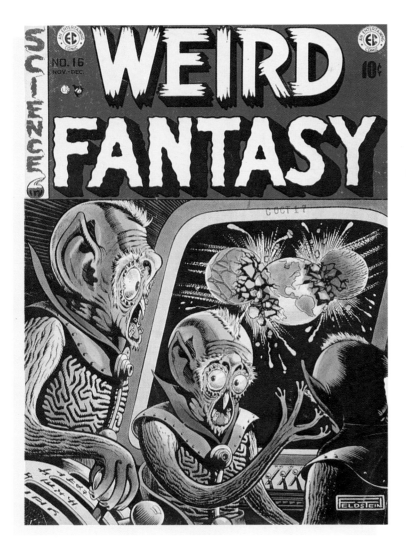

 Rare titles, such as Weird Fantasy, can often be found at comic book conventions at reasonable rates by collectors who know how to "work" a con to their advantage.

1978
Françoise Mouly and Art Spiegelman publish the first issue of *RAW*. Spiegelman's Maus is printed as a tiny supplement attached to the staples at the center of each issue. *RAW* would later become the first comic book to be sold through a major bookstore chain.

Conventions cut across all social boundaries to become the ultimate meeting place for all who make up the world of comic books (publishers, professionals, dealers, collectors, and fans). Joining together in a central location gives collectors enormous advantages they might not have otherwise. Very few beginning collectors have walked away from their first conventions unfulfilled, dissatisfied, or without a feeling of euphoria. Beginning with the initial wait in line on through to the convention's closing, one finds an atmosphere of unity; there is a common bond, a togetherness that the convention-goers most likely will not find to such a degree anywhere else.

Oftentimes, worthless comics, such as Gary Dunaier's Invisoworld, a bizarre experiment featuring no art, are showcased at cons as specialty items by unscrupulous dealers hoping to unload them on unsuspecting buyers.

Friendships and contacts can sometimes start while one is in line waiting for the doors to open. Serious collectors usually get to conventions early (especially if the convention is a large one where the turnout is expected to be huge) so they can get in and move about freely for a few minutes before the coming crush of fans makes it difficult. A beginning collector should get to a major "con" at least one hour before the doors open. One should not think of the upcoming wait as a waste of time but as an opportunity to network, or at least to gab and make new friends. If other collectors are "talking product" or discussing what is going to occur during the convention, a beginner should definitely try to join in the conversation. You have

1978
Eclipse Enterprises releases *Sabre* by Paul Gulacy, the first graphic album produced for the direct-sales market. This publication also initiates the policy of paying royalties and granting copyrights to comic book creators.

1981

Alan Moore begins his onslaught on the comic book industry with his contributions to Britain's *2000 A.D.* Among his work for the publication is the hilarious *D. R. & Quinch.*

1981

Jack Kirby begins his battle with Marvel Comics for the return of the original art he has created for the company. The total is estimated at 13,000 pages.

1982

After having the story rejected in 1981, Frank Miller is given the OK by Marvel Comics brass to present his frighteningly realistic look at drug abuse in the pages of *Daredevil, Nos. 182* through *184*. The story line guest-stars The Punisher. It quickly becomes a monstrous success.

nothing to lose and everything to gain.

Many of those waiting in line may have showed up just to meet with a certain artist or writer with whom they have a previously established rapport. Seasoned collectors have often cemented their reputation with dealers at conventions. Seasoned collectors will often take a beginner under their wing, helping them develop a working rapport with dealers who frequent regional cons. They will also do the same with any of the professional writers, artists, and editors they know that a beginning collector would like to meet. Not all seasoned collectors are looking to guide beginners along, but all were beginners once, and many are more than happy to lend a helping hand.

Also, the specialty shop a collector frequents will often rent a table at a convention. Depending on the relationship the collector has with that specialty shop, the collector may be given the chance to meet with their contacts.

PACK LIGHTLY

Collectors should always bring along only the items they wish to sell or know they will have the opportunity to get signed, since what is brought will have to be carried for the duration of the con. Many times, excess comics carried along have been sold for a considerable amount below their normal asking price simply because their owner has tired of carrying them. As if this were not enough, one should also consider that carrying comics from one's collection as well as merchandise bought at a convention can cause wear and damage to the comics.

Cons have been called malls of competing specialty shops, but that is only part of what makes up a comic book convention. Most promoters will pay at least one or two professional artists, writers, or editors to appear at their show just to boost attendance. Usually the professional will speak from a stage or podium or engage in a panel conference or debate with other professionals (or both at different times during the con), take questions from the audience, and then hold an autograph session. Often artists will work cons to sell their sketches or original art. A piece purchased cheaply from a talented beginner can skyrocket in value when that beginner suddenly becomes hot. Interaction between fans and professionals is important to the success of a convention. And it is important to point out that the pros of today were the fans of yesterday.

Sometimes some comic book companies will give previews or slide shows of upcoming releases to whet consumer appetites. Movie companies often preview film trailers of movie releases featuring comic book characters; Batman, Superman, The Punisher, and Captain America all got this kind of push in recent years.

Promoters will also sponsor costume and trivia contests and offer lucrative prizes to attract attention. (It is advised, however, that a fan carry his costume to a convention and put it on once inside. The humiliation and embarrassment in store for the adolescent wearing a super-hero suit in the streets is not worth the telling.) Auctions can often be beneficial to collectors who take part in them. Many times items going for high prices at the dealer tables will be sold for a small sum at an auction because of lack of interest.

Another good reason to go to cons is the exhibitions. Exhibits of older or very valuable merchandise (rare comics and artwork, for instance) are set up in museum-like rooms, enabling collectors to view first-hand items they might never have seen otherwise.

CLASSICS ILLUSTRATED are adaptations of the world's greatest works of literature, produced by some of the world's most talented writers and artists. Each lavishly illustrated volume is an accurate representation of the original work — distinctive, fresh and innovative, yet faithful to the book and true to the intentions of the author.

There are reasons why the original works are classics: Each is unique, each has weathered the test of time, and each continues to reflect and address the undying spirit of humanity in today's world. CLASSICS ILLUSTRATED reflect those individual styles that made the original works great — not just the stories, but the nuances as well. These adaptations naturally are abridged, but care has been taken to maintain the narrative sweep and as much of the original dialogue and narration as possible.

While they stand on their own merits, CLASSICS ILLUSTRATED are not substitutes for the originals. Rather, they are artistic interpretations, perfect introductions to an exciting world of remarkable ideas and unlimited possibilities — the world of great literature.

TO VINNY WITH my BEST WISHES

1982
The first direct-sales-only, regular continuing titles from a major comic book publisher are *Moon Knight*, *Ka-Zar the Savage*, and *The Micronauts* (all from Marvel Comics). This leads to a burgeoning market of comic book specialty shops.

1982
DC Comics debuts *Camelot 3000* by writer Mike W. Barr and artist Brian Bolland. It is the first self-contained story to be presented in a twelve-issue run. It also marks the first time a major comic book publisher would use new paper and printing methods to market a title.

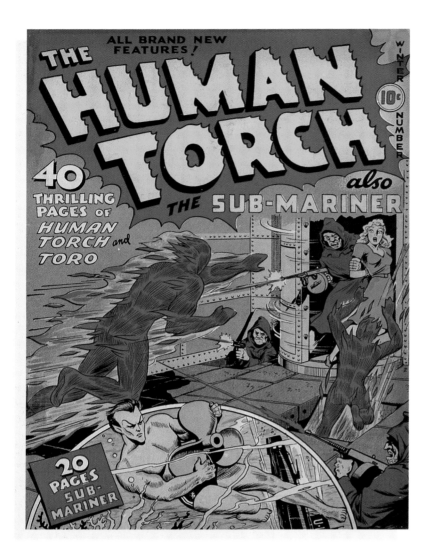

Crossovers, traditionally used as marketing ploy to increase sales of a title, have been around for decades (as is evident by the golden age issue of The Human Torch *which featured a guest appearance by the* Sub-Mariner).

Also, aspiring artists and writers can use conventions as a means of confronting professionals for criticism of their work. Editors can give advice as to how one goes about obtaining work in the field.

THE HEART OF THE CON

Ultimately, though, the heart of all conventions is the dealer's rooms. Convention dealers usually travel from con to con or, as is sometimes the case, along with a convention if it is traveling around the country. Many will have rarer items for sale than are found in local neighborhood specialty shops. Older comics, hard-to-find merchandise, small distribution independent comics, and fanzines not sold at neighborhood stores are often found at cons. Dealers usually also maintain mail-order companies on the side, so conventions are a good place for beginning collectors looking to establish relationships. Simply by asking, a beginning collector can find out how a particular dealer operates and what he or she is looking for. First impressions made while dealing are important and may lead to further business. Dealers will often hand over their card and store (or home) phone number along with the cash decided on for a transaction, all based on their first dealings with a new customer.

Haggling is a common sight at conventions. It is wise for a collector looking to purchase a specific item to wait until nearly the end of the convention, when the crowds have significantly died down, to haggle. A dealer, looking to pack up, will often take less money to get rid of an item to avoid having to pack it up and take it home. Of course, one runs the risk of waiting too long and losing the item in question to another collector with more money and a greater need. But then, that is all part of playing the game.

The dates and sites of conventions can be found in trade magazines, fanzines, and comic books and are posted in local specialty shops and some outside-the-market media (newspapers, magazines, signs in windows of local stores).

There are a multitude of different types and sizes of conventions, ranging from those housed in storefronts or small halls to those housed in large ballrooms or arenas. Admission prices usually coincide with the size of the venue and number of professionals appearing. Smaller conventions have an admission price of anywhere from $1 on up; larger ones featuring a multitude of celebrities and activities can fetch an admission price of up to $20.

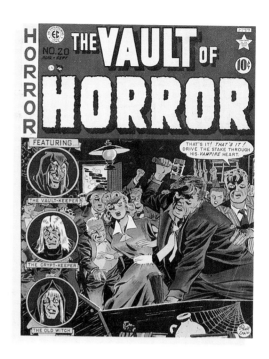

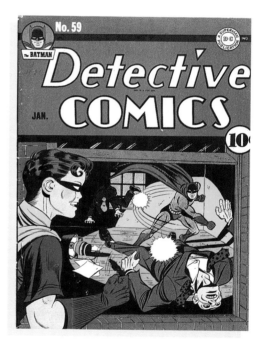

One of the main attractions at larger cons are the special appearances made by comic book writers and artists. Promoters will invest a great deal of money to fly in celebrities, put them up at hotels, and pay them to put in an appearance, in the hope that they will bring in a large crowd. Comics usually increase in value when autographed by their composers, but there is an art to acquiring signatures.

If the professional is only going to be signing autographs at a table, then it is best for a collector to be in line after the fifth person waiting but within the first few dozen. Most professionals need time to settle in, which usually affects the legibility of their first few autographs. On the other hand, after the first two or three dozen people have confronted the professional, he will usually become tired and scribble his name to get his job done. Remember, the legibility of an autograph is of the utmost importance when it comes to resale.

If a pro takes part in a panel or lecture, the collector should try to get as close to the front of the line as possible. Professionals usually come off the stage upbeat and ready to meet with fans.

No matter what the popularity level is of the professional signing, a collector should bring a minimal amount of merchandise for autographs. A collector should never bog down pros with numerous items to sign or pester them to provide free sketches.

When approaching the table where a pro is signing autographs, you should hold your book open to the page you wish to have signed, passing it along accordingly. There is nothing more frustrating to a professional than an inconsiderate fan who takes up valuable time choosing the page he wishes to have signed at the last minute, then hesitantly passes the book along while everyone waits.

A collector should always be polite, no matter how obnoxious a given professional might be. When confronting pros, it is best to kill them with kindness, so that you can get the signatures you desire.

A collector should always get his books signed on the front cover or the title page. It is important *never* to get a signature across pertinent art. It is all right to get autographs dated, but *not* personalized. It is nearly impossible to resell personal autographs. (Burt is not going to want a book personally autographed to Ann Marie.)

When walking away from the table, hold the book open to the signed page for a few moments. Most pros use black or silver markers, which can cause pages to stick together or smudge if they are not given time to dry.

Publicity fliers for the event (showcase or convention) are a good means of documenting a signing. Collectors can fold a copy and place it inside the book signed. It is advisable to keep it away from the autograph, usually inside the back cover.

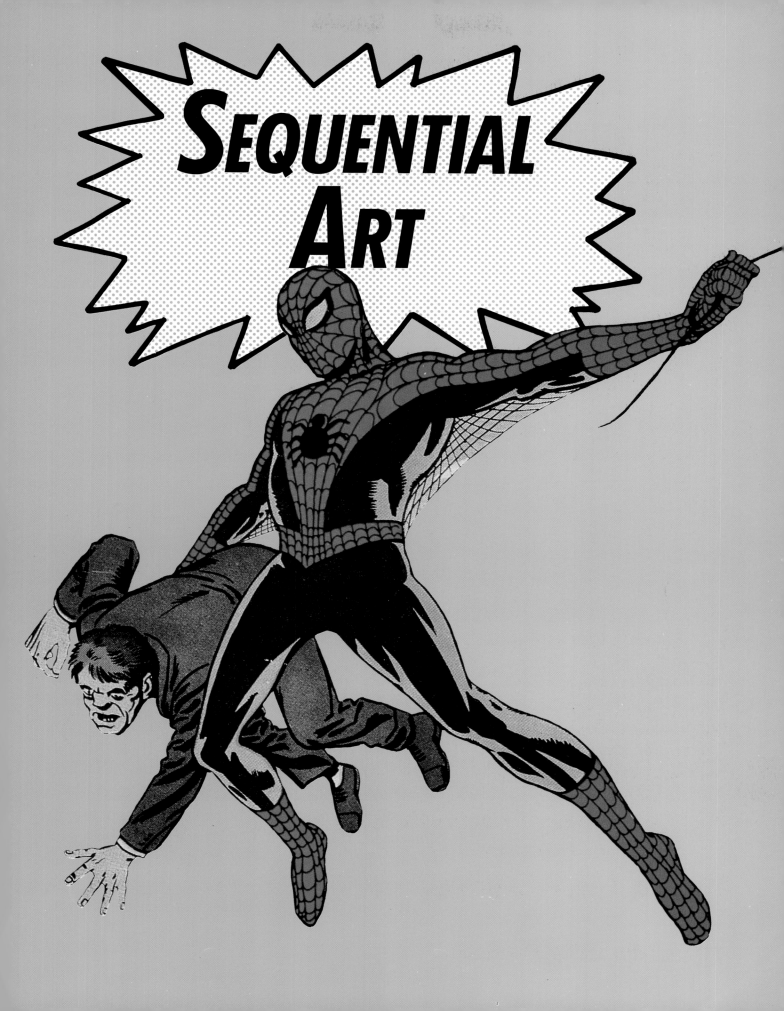

ix/12

1983
More comic book companies, aside from DC Comics and Marvel Comics, issue more titles than had been issued in the past forty years, with most independent comics relying on direct sales.

Comic book art in the eighties has finally come into its own, gaining respect and the well-deserved reputation of being a true art form. It is one of the few native American art forms, along with jazz and the musical. It has only recently been noted as an abstract art form since most comic book art is comprised of figures outlined with black ink; people are not one-dimensional, at least not physically, and do not have black-lined borders.

Art galleries and museums now frequently put original comic book art on exhibit. Comic book art has matured to the point where it has now earned the sophisticated moniker: ''sequential art.''

Comic book pioneer Will Eisner has been credited with

Golden age artwork, such as pages from **Action Comics**, have enjoyed new popularity as showpieces and collectibles, traveling around the country in exhibitions.

originally coining the term, which literally means "multi-panel or frame art" characterized by a regular or continuing story. And as with all forms of art, it has become a collector's market all its own, commanding top dollar for the work of the form's best talent.

PRICES

The price of comic book art ranges from nothing to amounts comparable with other contemporary forms of art. Pages that have actually been printed have more potential of becoming popular—read valuable—than ones that have not. Pages of pencils often do not receive as much as the same page will once it has been inked (that

1983
Ronin, a miniseries by Frank Miller, appears demonstrating martial arts and swordplay reminiscent of popular Japanese comic books of the 1970s and the revolutionary sequential art of France. But its complex story line and highly erratic publication schedule ultimately would make it unsuccessful.

price increasing if the page has also been lettered and finished). Of course, the simplest sketch by a recognized professional will bring top dollar as long as the pro is still ''hot.''

Sequential art can be found in art galleries, at conventions, and through the classified advertisements in various trade magazines. Some dealers sell their pages through postings in specialty shops and by word of mouth through store managers. Some artists sell pages of their books through ads in the comics themselves.

An original sequential art collection is potentially lucrative. Art dealing is a tricky business. Given the speed with which comic artists can rise and fall in popularity, one should give serious consideration before making such investments.

SKETCHES

One of the attractions at major comic book conventions are the live shows of one or more comic artists at work. Most of the time, these artists will produce many sketches, most of which will stay in the hands of the fans, sometimes for a fee, sometimes for free.

If you buy the sketch, don't hesitate to resell it for a profit. But if you get it for free, don't sell it —at least not at the same convention. You might offend the artist. Case in point: Frank Frazetta, one of the most easygoing professionals in the comics field, was approached for a sketch by a collector at a convention. The fan made his plea for the sketch in the hotel restaurant (the convention was held in the hotel's ballroom) during Frazetta's meal. Despite the fan's bad timing, the artist grabbed a napkin and did a quick drawing of a barbarian, which he presented to the collector free of charge. Several hours later, Frazetta found the napkin for sale in the dealers' room for $60. The fan had sold it for $40 and left the convention. Needless to say, there have not been too many free Frank Frazetta pieces distributed lately, and justifiably so.

1985
The first major exhibition of sequential or comic book art is held from May 19 through August 2 at Ohio State University's Library of Communication and Graphic arts.

The first issue of Spider-Man, yet another monthly title featuring the arachknight, was one of the biggest selling single comic issues of all time. That feat was later topped by X-Force #1 and then by X-Men #1. All of these issues were released in multiple formats.

1985
During the fiftieth anniversary year of DC Comics, a miniseries entitled *Crisis on Infinite Earths* is released with the intention of simplifying and revitalizing the DC universe. Mainstay Supergirl and the original Flash are killed during the series.

Many collectors take the storage of their books for granted at first, only to discover later their once valuable books have become discolored and weathered.

Smaller, specialized collections can be neatly placed in albums or binders with transparent pockets. Great for bookshelves, these materials can be found in art stores, comic book specialty shops, and some large stationery stores. Binders usually have pockets on their spines for listing contents, indexing, or alphabetizing according to the specifics of your collection.

The downside of using binders to maintain a collection is the cost or overhead eventually created as a collection grows. Binders or albums are usually able to carry no more than twenty to twenty-five issues, a problem for collectors with limited funds. Most collectors choose to use cardboard boxes, clear plastic sleeves, and backing boards.

Acid-free, two-ply cardboard boxes cost a few cents more than cardboard boxes found at no cost at any supermarket or delicatessen but are an important part of maintaining a collection. The acids found in regular cardboard boxes will cause a comic book's paper to discolor, diminishing the luster of its cover.

Standard comic book boxes and lids, easy to assemble, do not require any fittings and will house most present-day-format books as well as some golden- and silver-age comic books. Oversized comic books can usually be stored in magazine-size boxes.

Comic book boxes usually come in three sizes: long (holding up to 350 books), short (up to 200 books), and magazine-size (up to 100 oversized comics or magazines). After properly packaging a comic book, store it upright. You should fill your boxes without overstuffing. If there is excess room left after you arrange your books, insert a divider card and fill the space with crumbled, virgin-white paper or cut up an additional cardboard box and use the pieces as a wedge in the space. Be sure not to create any unnecessary stress points or creases.

BAG YOUR PURCHASE

Comic book bags are important for helping a comic book retain its current grade or condition. Comic book bags (sometimes referred to as sleeves or covers) shield the book from the many outside elements that might damage it. There are a variety of different materials used to produce comic bags (Mylar and polyethylene, for example), but while some types of comic book bags are cheaper than others, the one most recommended is the Mylar Comic Book Sleeve (Mylar is a trademark of the DuPont Com-

1986
DC Comics attracts widespread attention with John Byrne's revision and direction changes of *Superman*.

1986
DC Comics releases Frank Miller's *The Dark Knight Returns*, a miniseries that reworks as well as revitalizes the character of Batman, whose sales had been floundering since the late 1970s. The success of this miniseries as well as the media attention it garners, help to convince critics that comic books have finally grown up.

1986
Writer Alan Moore and artist Dave Gibbon create *The Watchmen*, an intelligent, realistic look at super heroes living with the threat of nuclear war. It is released as a maxiseries by DC Comics and comes to be hailed by most critics and readers as one of the finest single works ever produced in the field of comics.

1987

Marvel Comics comes to an agreement with Jack Kirby and returns 2,100 pages to him in return for the copyright and ownership of the characters he created for them.

1987

First Comics launches the translated reprints of popular Japanese comics with *Lone Wolf & Cub*. Marvel Comics follows with *Akira*.

1987

Pantheon publishes a book edition of Art Spiegelman's *Maus: A Survivor's Tale*. It is later nominated for the National Book Critics Circle Award in Biography, the first comic book to be so honored.

pany). It is important to remember that comic book bags should be replaced every two to three years, as the aging plastic may lose its ability to protect the comic it houses.

Backing boards are important for maintaining the rigidness of the issue while in storage. Backing boards help enhance the appearance of a comic book for presentation, by keeping the issue flat and neat.

Although one can purchase short-term boards (which contain small amounts of acids) at a cheaper price, an investment in slightly more expensive all-white, acid-free boards is highly recommended. These boards can usually be obtained in two sizes: silver-age ($7''$ x $10\frac{1}{2}''$) and standard ($6\frac{3}{4}''$ x $10\frac{1}{4}''$).

The proper procedure for inserting backing boards is easy, but must be done carefully. Sliding the board until it reaches the bottom, straighten out the back by gently moving it until the bag is flat and all sides and edges coincide with the backing board. Slip the issue inside, upside down with the front cover to the inside lip, without bending or tearing the pages. Leaving about one-eighth of an inch perimeter around the comic, straighten the issue and fold the lip over. By now the lip should be folded over the bottom half of the back cover. If so, pull the lip over tightly without harming the enclosed comic book and place a small piece of tape across lip and bag.

Divider cards for partitioning different portions of a collection are available in both cardboard and plastic, but neither is much better though the plastic divider cards are more rigid. Depending on the relationship you have with the manager or owner of the specialty shop you frequent, you may be able to get comic-book-company-supplied, graphically designed divider cards. They are usually packed inside the cartons along with each week's new comic book releases, only to be tossed out when not needed by the store.

If you have several books you wish to keep exposed on a shelf or mantel, you can buy adjustable easels or stands. They are perfect for displaying comic books, magazines, and other formats. Since these publications are left out in the open, the elements will affect the sleeves that protect them more quickly, making it necessary to change the bags every six to eight months. Easels are becoming more popular as cover art is being recognized as a true art form. Easels are also being used to display counter or viewable copies of special format books in specialty shops. (Please, however, do not ignore the highly destructive effects of direct sunlight, against which no comic is safe.)

Comic book boxes, sleeves, backing boards, binders, albums, and easels are obtainable at comic book specialty shops, art stores, some larger stationery stores, and by mail order. When ordering an item through the mail, it is sometimes cheaper to buy in lots or increments (usually in multiples of 50 or 100). The price per item will decrease as the amount purchased increases.

Then, once a collection is properly wrapped and boxed, it must be stored. The ideal conditions for storing a collection are a cool, dry atmosphere, a temperature of between 40 and 50°F, and a relative humidity of about 50 percent. Air-conditioning is recommended if available. Books should be stored away from excessive dampness, dust, air pollution, and ultraviolet light. Tungsten filament light is ideal for viewing comic books. You should keep your collection away from any source of excessive heat (radiators, hot water pipes, steam pipes) to prevent yellowing and weathering of the pages.

Remember, there are acids left in most comic books that will lead to aging, yellowing, and discoloring. Improper storage will only accelerate this process.

1988
"The Killing Joke," a classic Batman story that reworks the origin of The Joker, is released after a four-year wait. Written by Alan Moore with art by Brian Bolland, "Killing Joke's" first printing sells out instantly.

1988
During the celebration of his fiftieth birthday, Superman becomes the first comic book character to appear on the cover of *Time* magazine. An hour-long, prime-time television special about Superman airs during February on CBS.

The proper handling of comic books, as well as overall proper care, will help keep decades-old comics such as Weird Fantasy, *in their original, store bought condition.*

1988

After a close phone-in poll, the second Robin, Jason Todd, is killed off by The Joker during issues 426 through 429 of *Batman*, a miniseries within a series subtitled "A Death in the Family." This would mark the first time that comic book fans have their say on the fate of a major character. Batman creator Bob Kane is deeply disturbed by the poll's outcome.

HANDLING VALUABLE COMIC BOOKS

Carefully remove the seal and slide the comic book out of its sleeve, making sure the pages do not tear, bend, or come in contact with any sticky surface left by the seal. The original comic should then be laid on the palm of one *dry* hand so it stays relatively flat and secure. Then, flip or slightly roll back the pages with the thumb and forefinger. When replacing the book, make sure not to bend or tear its edges or corners, and reseal the sleeve.

You should make sure that your hands are not sweaty

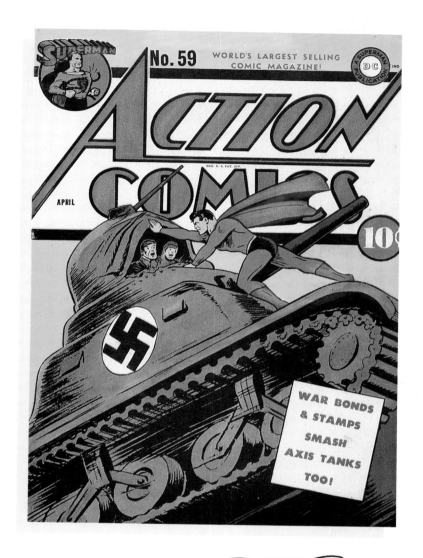

Golden age comics which capitalized on the support of the American cause in World War II, such as Action Comics No. 59, are the current rage among collectors dealing in older issues.

while handling the books. Oils from your skin will smudge or soil the cover.

There is special document tape available, which is guaranteed not to brown or damage with age, should one wish to mend a tear in a cover or page of a comic book. It is not highly recommended by most dealers and collectors, who view tape repairs as further damage and will downgrade a comic book's value accordingly.

If you take all the points discussed in this chapter into account and properly handle, store, and maintain your collection, it will eventually reciprocate the gesture in the future by staying in relatively mint condition.

1988

Comic books enter the computer age. After the success of the first computer-generated comic book, *Shatter,* Marvel Comics releases "the state of the art" graphic novel, *Crash,* featuring Iron Man. In 1990, the technology used to create *Crash* would become obsolete with the release of the graphic novel *Digital Justice* featuring Batman. Today, most standard-format comics are computer-colorized.

PERSONAL CARE

Not everyone wants to wheel and deal. Many people collect comics simply because they like to read them and they see no sense in throwing one away just because they've finished reading it.

Comics are fun. People shouldn't be made to feel small or stupid because they like having boxes of comics. There are comics for every taste, every age, and every sensibility. If somebody likes to read comics then they should do so out in the open, without being ashamed. Indeed, most of the time when someone ridicules a comic reader in public, it only takes a small bit of conversation between the two to convince the non-reader that there are plenty of comics available which he or she might enjoy. Someone who laughs at a fan for reading Batman today might tomorrow find him or herself being laughed at for reading *Reid Fleming, World's Toughest Milkman,* or *The Bradleys,* or any of the hundreds of other alternative titles attracting new readers.

This is not to say that the non-business-oriented collector should disregard the advice in the rest of this book. Thousands of casual collectors have later on decided to stop collecting comics, or to sell part or all of their collections. Sometimes a need for money has forced fans to sell books with which they thought they would never part. Sadly there is a multitude of reasons that can force someone to liquidate a collection.

The point here is, even if you have no intention of ever selling any of your comics, you should still care for them properly. Look books over on the rack before buying them. Why take the one with the off-center cover, or bad stapling, or the distributor's packing notes written across the title? Always take the best one on the rack. Always protect each book as if it were going to be sold.

There is no law that says one must buy everything that comes out or constantly speculate on what will happen in the marketplace. It is common sense that books in good condition will sell for more than those in bad condition. Those with limited funds who *know* they are *never* going to sell their books, who wish only to maintain a collection for fun and personal fulfillment, can have titles bound professionally. Those willing to contemplate the idea of sales at some time in the future can at least take *some* steps to be prepared. They can get cardboard boxes in any grocery store or supermarket at no cost. For most new comic books, quart-sized bleach boxes are usually ideal. Additional boxes can be cut into squares slightly larger than the comics to place behind every ten or so issues to keep them firm and upright. Storing these boxes as one would a collection meant for investment and resale will not damage anyone's integrity as a collector, but it will protect a collection. And twenty years later, whether a person wants to sell the books, or just read them again, at least the collection will still be intact so either is an option (though the books may have deteriorated some because of chemicals in the boxes).

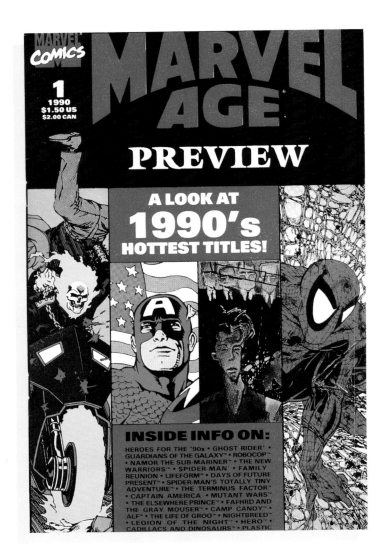

Marvel Age *is a standard comic-book-size preview magazine that once featured only upcoming Marvel products. Filled with interviews of Marvel staff and in-depth looks at special releases, this once free magazine now costs money. Title-by-title previews of Marvel Comics are now housed exclusively in Marvel Requirer.*

1989
After months of hype, the movie *Batman* opens in June to record-setting crowds and becomes the fastest film in history to break the $300 million box-office barrier. It settles in as the fifth largest grossing film of all time. It also comes out on video after theatrical release faster than any previous hit film.

Staying on top of current market swings (trends, hype, what's hot, what's not) requires hard work. There are guides to help collectors of all degrees make predictions and invest their money wisely: They are, of course, "the trades."

Genre-related trades are a news service for everyone in the comic book market (collectors, dealers, specialty shop owners, professionals, publishers), keeping them updated on all current happenings. There are a variety of trades available. Some are little more than commercial catalogs or self-indulgent fanzines, but some do have intelligent insights to offer on the many products in the market.

The **Dark Horse Insider** *is a comic book specialty-shop-only free flier that advertises and previews Dark Horse products. Dark Horse is known for its adaptations of the movies Predator and Aliens.*

THE GUIDES

There is a multitude of comic book genre-related magazines currently on the market (many which are only available on a regional basis), too numerous to mention here; accordingly, the following alphabetical list is comprised of the more popular (or more widely available) titles.

ADVANCE COMICS A monthly catalog detailing the comic book-related merchandise to be released in upcoming months. Each product listed comes along with a paragraph of text previewing the item. The downside of this format is that the text is always positive (since the

1989
Arkham Asylum, a fully painted graphic novel featuring Batman, is released after an extended delay. Despite a cover price of $25, it would become the first comic book to exceed $2.5 million in advance sales. Some critics say you need a college degree to even come close to understanding it.

The Marvel Requirer *is a comic book specialty shop handout that contains previews of upcoming releases. But unlike* Marvel Age, *it contains no major interviews or previews and is ''free.''*

magazine is indeed a catalog), never giving any criticism of any product listed. Only the seasoned collector has the necessary experience to see through the propaganda. Beginners should only look at magazines such as *Advance Comics* as a preview of upcoming releases and be careful not to get caught up in any hype. The cover price of the magazine is minimal, though many specialty shop owners and dealers will hand them over to customers at no charge hoping to attract further business.

AMAZING HEROES   Published twice monthly by Fantagraphics books, this is one of the better trade magazines currently available, offering hot news, in-depth inter-

1990
Current estimates put the annual revenue taken in by the comic industry at over $400 million.

> **Amazing Heroes** *offers news about many independents that are often overshadowed by the larger publishers, so it's a good source for people who collect comics from the smaller companies.*

views with pertinent professionals, articles on market trends, objective reviews and criticism, humor, and satire. *Amazing Heroes* also covers many independents that are often overshadowed by the larger publishers, making it worthwhile to collectors who fancy smaller comic book companies.

COMICS BUYER'S GUIDE
A weekly trade newspaper that is the Bible of all comic book genre-related magazines. It features up-to-the-minute news, comprehensive listings of shows and conventions, articles containing valuable information to collectors of all levels,

1990
A graphic anthology entitled *Breakthrough* is released in early spring. A contribution by the comic book community to the worldwide celebration marking the falling of the Berlin Wall, the book features the reaction (in graphic shorts or sequential art) of twenty-seven notable professionals.

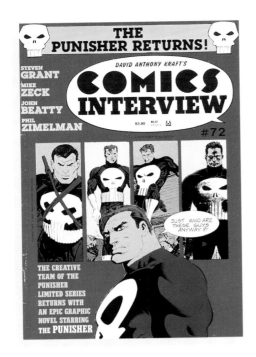

a multitude of advertisements from a nationwide scope of specialty shops, convention dealers, and mail-order companies, as well as an extensive classified listing for collectors to search for and deal items. *Comic Buyer's Guide* is sold at most larger specialty shops though subscriptions are available at discount prices.

A supplemental price guide is periodically released and features most titles of value from the mid-1950s to the present.

COMICS INTERVIEW
A trade magazine that is exactly what it says it is, a series of comics-related interviews. Recent issues have usually revolved around a single character or theme. For instance, issue 72 featured The Punisher and many of the artists and writers who have handled the character. Published monthly by Fictioneer Books, Ltd.

COMICS JOURNAL
Subtitled "the magazine of news and criticism," it is just that. Offbeat, *Comics Journal* offers a different perspective on the usual articles, reviews, and news stories found in the other genre trades. It takes an honest, almost cynical look at the comic book market and holds nothing back. Most important, it takes itself seriously and offers better, and better-written, articles than its competition. Published by Fantagraphics Books, the *Comics Journal* is usually available monthly.

COMICS SCENE
Originally *Comics World* (it changed its title just before the premiere issue was released when it was learned that there was another *Comics World*, a small fanzine with minimal distribution), *Comics Scene* covers the higher profile releases and happenings in the comic market. Published bimonthly by Starlog Communication International, Inc. *(Starlog, Fangoria, Gorezone),* recent issues of *Comics Scene* have

Comic Shop News *is a weekly newspaper that offers up-to-the-minute news, interviews, and previews of future releases of all comic-book-related merchandise.*

previewed genre-related films such as *Batman*, *Captain America*, and *Teenage Mutant Ninja Turtles*.

COMIC SHOP NEWS   Published weekly by Para-Graphics, *Comic Shop News* is a specialty shop handout that features up-to-the-minute happenings in the world of comics and serves as the one of the better vehicles for the collector to predict trends. One of the features, CSN Hot Picks!, previews a few dozen of the more important releases in a given month.

1990
After an extended absence, *Classics Illustrated Comics* returns, copublished by First Comics and Berkeley. Among the initial issues are *Moby Dick* adapted by Bill Sienkiewicz, *Through the Looking Glass* adapted by Kyle Baker, and *Great Expectations* adapted by Rick Geary. This would be the first time an independent comic book company would copublish a series of comics with a major comic book company.

DC'S COMING COMICS *AND* DC'S DIRECT CURRENTS

Specialty shop handouts that preview upcoming DC Comics releases and give tentative shipping dates. *Direct Currents* is a monthly standard-size flier that also features the reprinting of a classic comic cover and profiles one of the company's professionals. *Coming Comics*, which is similar in content, is printed in a larger format on a heavy paper stock. Unlike *Direct Currents*, *Coming Comics* has no classic covers or articles, but does feature upcoming releases from its subsidiary Piranha Press and the independent company Comico Inc., which DC also distributes. It also lists more expensive formats such as graphic novels and trade paperbacks, which are also available through back order.

MARVEL AGE MAGAZINE

Originally presented in the same format as DC Comics' *Direct Currents*, *Marvel Age* is now presented in a standard-size format and contains previews of the month's releases. It also contains related articles, interviews, continuing columns *(The Mutant Report)*, and retrospectives. Unlike DC's fliers, *Marvel Age Magazine* costs $1 and is now available at newsstands as well as through direct-sales channels.

OVERSTREET COMIC BOOK PRICE GUIDE

The best known and respected of the many price guides on the market today. Published by The House Of Collectibles, the Overstreet price guide lists most comics of any value. *Overstreet Comic Book Price Guide Companion* and *Overstreet's Price Update* are also available to update any changes in the market price of a title.

OTHER MAGS

One of the many ways to predict trends or market swings comes from studying the way magazines and newspapers that do not normally give space to comics react to certain genre-related happenings. The attention comes from all avenues and media, from rock-and-roll magazines to daily newspapers, and it serves as a sign to where the market is going and how a collector should invest his money.

Many of the horror genre's magazines, *Fangoria, Toxic Shock, Gorezone,* and *Slaughter House,* have begun giving regular attention in the form of reviews, articles, and interviews to horror comics. Not surprisingly, horror comics are on the rise once more, with the reprinting of EC Comics titles from the 1950s, DC's adult horror line, and the various Clive Barker titles currently gracing comic shop racks.

Twilight Zone and *Midnight Graffiti* have featured articles on dark fantasy comics, and *Gateways,* a magazine that covers the world of role-playing games, has featured profiles and dossiers of many popular comic book characters for the purpose of entering them into games. The coverage of the characters featured in *Gateways—*

The X-Men, Wolverine, and The Punisher—came just as the popularity of each character began to skyrocket.

Premiere, a magazine dedicated to filmdom, frequently features exposés on comic book characters headed to the big screen. Among them: Swamp Thing, Teenage Mutant Ninja Turtles, and, of course, Batman. The hype given to a character will usually ensure at least a brief rise in the value of its title's run.

Many rock-and-roll magazines, which cover the world of music and pop culture, frequently cover comic book titles. *Kerrang,* a weekly English heavy metal magazine available in many record shops, occasionally runs articles on comics. Recently it ran articles on *Rock-and-Roll Comics* and Clive Barker discussing his projects.

Newspapers such as *The New York Times, The New York Daily News, The Los Angeles Times,* and *Village Voice* have run stories on comics and their effects—usually on the heels of a trend. As the Teenage Mutant Ninja Turtles gained in popularity, *The News* ran an article on them; a market boom followed. The boom was not caused by the article, rather it was predicted by it.

RECENT HISTORY

1991—Sotheby's Holdings Inc. held its first-ever comic-book auction, but blamed on the recession, books and artwork (such as a copy of the original *Marvel Comic*) sold well under expectations.

1992—The first issue of a second *X-Men* title (named, oddly enough "X-Men") sold a record seven million copies.

1992—Alpha Flight's Northstar became the first main character in a major comic company (Marvel) to reveal his homosexuality. The choice to deal with the subject was applauded. A month later, Marvel was forced to recall copies of N.F.L. Superstar for what was deemed an obvious biased depiction of Hopi Indians. As much as things change, they remain the same.

THE BEST-KNOWN COMIC BOOK COMPANIES

Archie Productions, Inc.
325 Fayette Avenue
Mamaroneck, NY 10543

Calibre Tome
31162 W. Warren Avenue
Westland, MI 48185

DC/Impact/Piranha Comics, Inc.
1325 Avenue of the Americas
New York, NY 10019

Dark Horse Comics
10956 S.E. Main Street
Milwaukee, OR 97222

Eclipse Enterprises
P.O. Box 1099
Forestville, CA 95436

Fleetway/Quality
P.O. Box 4569
Toms River, NJ 08754

Kitchen Sink Press
#2 Swamp Road
Princeton, WI 54968

Marvel/Epic
387 Park Avenue South
New York, NY 10016

Eternity/Malibu/Aircel
5321 Sterling Center Drive
Westlake Village, CA 91361

Fantagraphics Books
7563 Lake City Way
Seattle, WA 98115

Gladstone Publishing, Ltd.
P.O. Box 2079
Prescott, AZ 86302

Harvey Publications, Inc.
4115 Radford Avenue
Studio City, CA 91604

Innovation Publishing
3622 Jacob Street
Wheeling, WV 26003

Jademan (Holdings) Ltd.
28/F.
Harbour Centre,
25, Harbour Road
Hong Kong

Rip Off Press Inc.
P.O. Box 4686
Auburn, CA 95604

Tundra Publishing
320 Riverside Dr.
Northampton, MA 01060

Vortex Comics
P.O. Box 77010
San Francisco, CA 94107

INDEX